BOB DYLAN
100 SONGS

Simon & Schuster

New York   London   Toronto   Sydney   New Delhi

Simon & Schuster
1230 Avenue of the Americas
New York, NY 10020

First Simon & Schuster trade paperback edition October 2017

SIMON & SCHUSTER and colophon are registered trademarks of Simon & Schuster, Inc.

For information about special discounts for bulk purchases, please contact Simon & Schuster Special Sales at 1-866-506-1949 or business@simonandschuster.com.

The Simon & Schuster Speakers Bureau can bring authors to your live event. For more information or to book an event, contact the Simon & Schuster Speakers Bureau at 1-866-248-3049 or visit our website at www.simonspeakers.com.

Designed by Geoff Gans

Manufactured in the United States of America

10   9   8   7   6   5   4   3   2

Library of Congress Cataloging-in-Publication Data

Names: Dylan, Bob, 1941–
Title: 100 songs / by Bob Dylan.
Other titles: One hundred songs
Description: First Simon & Schuster trade paperback edition. | New York : Simon and Schuster,
2017. | Includes bibliographical references and index.
Identifiers: LCCN 2017026861 | ISBN 9781501173363 (trade pbk.)
Subjects: LCSH: Popular music—United States—Texts. | Songs, English—United States—Texts.
Classification: LCC ML54.6.D94 L97 2017 | DDC 781.630973—dc23 LC record available at
https://lccn.loc.gov/2017026861

ISBN 978-1-5011-7336-3
ISBN 978-1-5011-7337-0 (ebook)

THE SONGS

SONG TO WOODY

I'm out here a thousand miles from my home
Walkin' a road other men have gone down
I'm seein' your world of people and things
Your paupers and peasants and princes and kings

Hey, hey, Woody Guthrie, I wrote you a song
'Bout a funny ol' world that's a-comin' along
Seems sick an' it's hungry, it's tired an' it's torn
It looks like it's a-dyin' an' it's hardly been born

Hey, Woody Guthrie, but I know that you know
All the things that I'm a-sayin' an' a-many times more
I'm a-singin' you the song, but I can't sing enough
'Cause there's not many men that done the things that you've done

Here's to Cisco an' Sonny an' Leadbelly too
An' to all the good people that traveled with you
Here's to the hearts and the hands of the men
That come with the dust and are gone with the wind

I'm a-leavin' tomorrow, but I could leave today
Somewhere down the road someday
The very last thing that I'd want to do
Is to say I've been hittin' some hard travelin' too

BLOWIN' IN THE WIND

How many roads must a man walk down
Before you call him a man?
Yes, 'n' how many seas must a white dove sail
Before she sleeps in the sand?
Yes, 'n' how many times must the cannonballs fly
Before they're forever banned?
The answer, my friend, is blowin' in the wind
The answer is blowin' in the wind

How many years can a mountain exist
Before it's washed to the sea?
Yes, 'n' how many years can some people exist
Before they're allowed to be free?
Yes, 'n' how many times can a man turn his head
Pretending he just doesn't see?
The answer, my friend, is blowin' in the wind
The answer is blowin' in the wind

How many times must a man look up
Before he can see the sky?
Yes, 'n' how many ears must one man have
Before he can hear people cry?
Yes, 'n' how many deaths will it take till he knows
That too many people have died?
The answer, my friend, is blowin' in the wind
The answer is blowin' in the wind

GIRL OF THE NORTH COUNTRY

Well, if you're travelin' in the north country fair
Where the winds hit heavy on the borderline
Remember me to one who lives there
She once was a true love of mine

Well, if you go when the snowflakes storm
When the rivers freeze and summer ends
Please see if she's wearing a coat so warm
To keep her from the howlin' winds

Please see for me if her hair hangs long
If it rolls and flows all down her breast
Please see for me if her hair hangs long
That's the way I remember her best

I'm a-wonderin' if she remembers me at all
Many times I've often prayed
In the darkness of my night
In the brightness of my day

So if you're travelin' in the north country fair
Where the winds hit heavy on the borderline
Remember me to one who lives there
She once was a true love of mine

MASTERS OF WAR

Come you masters of war
You that build all the guns
You that build the death planes
You that build the big bombs
You that hide behind walls
You that hide behind desks
I just want you to know
I can see through your masks

You that never done nothin'
But build to destroy
You play with my world
Like it's your little toy
You put a gun in my hand
And you hide from my eyes
And you turn and run farther
When the fast bullets fly

Like Judas of old
You lie and deceive
A world war can be won
You want me to believe
But I see through your eyes
And I see through your brain
Like I see through the water
That runs down my drain

You fasten the triggers
For the others to fire
Then you set back and watch
When the death count gets higher
You hide in your mansion
As young people's blood
Flows out of their bodies

And is buried in the mud

You've thrown the worst fear
That can ever be hurled
Fear to bring children
Into the world
For threatening my baby
Unborn and unnamed
You ain't worth the blood
That runs in your veins

How much do I know
To talk out of turn
You might say that I'm young
You might say I'm unlearned
But there's one thing I know
Though I'm younger than you
Even Jesus would never
Forgive what you do

Let me ask you one question
Is your money that good
Will it buy you forgiveness
Do you think that it could
I think you will find
When your death takes its toll
All the money you made
Will never buy back your soul

And I hope that you die
And your death'll come soon
I will follow your casket
In the pale afternoon
And I'll watch while you're lowered
Down to your deathbed
And I'll stand o'er your grave

'Til I'm sure that you're dead

A HARD RAIN'S A-GONNA FALL

Oh, where have you been, my blue-eyed son?
Oh, where have you been, my darling young one?
I've stumbled on the side of twelve misty mountains
I've walked and I've crawled on six crooked highways
I've stepped in the middle of seven sad forests
I've been out in front of a dozen dead oceans
I've been ten thousand miles in the mouth of a graveyard
And it's a hard, and it's a hard, it's a hard, and it's a hard
And it's a hard rain's a-gonna fall

Oh, what did you see, my blue-eyed son?
Oh, what did you see, my darling young one?
I saw a newborn baby with wild wolves all around it
I saw a highway of diamonds with nobody on it
I saw a black branch with blood that kept drippin'
I saw a room full of men with their hammers a-bleedin'
I saw a white ladder all covered with water
I saw ten thousand talkers whose tongues were all broken
I saw guns and sharp swords in the hands of young children
And it's a hard, and it's a hard, it's a hard, it's a hard
And it's a hard rain's a-gonna fall

And what did you hear, my blue-eyed son?
And what did you hear, my darling young one?
I heard the sound of a thunder, it roared out a warnin'
Heard the roar of a wave that could drown the whole world
Heard one hundred drummers whose hands were a-blazin'
Heard ten thousand whisperin' and nobody listenin'

Heard one person starve, I heard many people laughin'
Heard the song of a poet who died in the gutter
Heard the sound of a clown who cried in the alley
And it's a hard, and it's a hard, it's a hard, it's a hard
And it's a hard rain's a-gonna fall

Oh, who did you meet, my blue-eyed son?
Who did you meet, my darling young one?
I met a young child beside a dead pony
I met a white man who walked a black dog
I met a young woman whose body was burning
I met a young girl, she gave me a rainbow
I met one man who was wounded in love
I met another man who was wounded with hatred
And it's a hard, it's a hard, it's a hard, it's a hard
It's a hard rain's a-gonna fall

Oh, what'll you do now, my blue-eyed son?
Oh, what'll you do now, my darling young one?
I'm a-goin' back out 'fore the rain starts a-fallin'
I'll walk to the depths of the deepest black forest
Where the people are many and their hands are all empty
Where the pellets of poison are flooding their waters
Where the home in the valley meets the damp dirty prison
Where the executioner's face is always well hidden
Where hunger is ugly, where souls are forgotten
Where black is the color, where none is the number
And I'll tell it and think it and speak it and breathe it
And reflect it from the mountain so all souls can see it
Then I'll stand on the ocean until I start sinkin'
But I'll know my song well before I start singin'
And it's a hard, it's a hard, it's a hard, it's a hard
It's a hard rain's a-gonna fall

DON'T THINK TWICE, IT'S ALL RIGHT

It ain't no use to sit and wonder why, babe
It don't matter, anyhow
An' it ain't no use to sit and wonder why, babe
If you don't know by now
When your rooster crows at the break of dawn
Look out your window and I'll be gone
You're the reason I'm trav'lin' on
Don't think twice, it's all right

It ain't no use in turnin' on your light, babe
That light I never knowed
An' it ain't no use in turnin' on your light, babe
I'm on the dark side of the road
Still I wish there was somethin' you would do or say
To try and make me change my mind and stay
We never did too much talkin' anyway
So don't think twice, it's all right

It ain't no use in callin' out my name, gal
Like you never did before
It ain't no use in callin' out my name, gal
I can't hear you anymore
I'm a-thinkin' and a-wond'rin' all the way down the road
I once loved a woman, a child I'm told
I give her my heart but she wanted my soul
But don't think twice, it's all right

I'm walkin' down that long, lonesome road, babe

Where I'm bound, I can't tell
But goodbye's too good a word, gal
So I'll just say fare thee well
I ain't sayin' you treated me unkind
You could have done better but I don't mind
You just kinda wasted my precious time
But don't think twice, it's all right

THE TIMES THEY ARE A-CHANGIN'

Come gather 'round people
Wherever you roam
And admit that the waters
Around you have grown
And accept it that soon
You'll be drenched to the bone
If your time to you is worth savin'
Then you better start swimmin' or you'll sink like a stone
For the times they are a-changin'

Come writers and critics
Who prophesize with your pen
And keep your eyes wide
The chance won't come again
And don't speak too soon
For the wheel's still in spin
And there's no tellin' who that it's namin'
For the loser now will be later to win
For the times they are a-changin'

Come senators, congressmen
Please heed the call
Don't stand in the doorway
Don't block up the hall
For he that gets hurt
Will be he who has stalled
There's a battle outside and it is ragin'
It'll soon shake your windows and rattle your walls
For the times they are a-changin'

Come mothers and fathers
Throughout the land
And don't criticize
What you can't understand
Your sons and your daughters

Are beyond your command
Your old road is rapidly agin'
Please get out of the new one if you can't lend your hand
For the times they are a-changin'

The line it is drawn
The curse it is cast
The slow one now
Will later be fast
As the present now
Will later be past
The order is rapidly fadin'
And the first one now will later be last
For the times they are a-changin'

BALLAD OF HOLLIS BROWN

Hollis Brown
He lived on the outside of town
Hollis Brown
He lived on the outside of town
With his wife and five children
And his cabin fallin' down

You looked for work and money
And you walked a rugged mile
You looked for work and money
And you walked a rugged mile
Your children are so hungry
That they don't know how to smile

Your baby's eyes look crazy
They're a-tuggin' at your sleeve
Your baby's eyes look crazy
They're a-tuggin' at your sleeve
You walk the floor and wonder why
With every breath you breathe

The rats have got your flour
Bad blood it got your mare
The rats have got your flour
Bad blood it got your mare
If there's anyone that knows
Is there anyone that cares?

You prayed to the Lord above
Oh please send you a friend
You prayed to the Lord above

Oh please send you a friend
Your empty pockets tell yuh
That you ain't a-got no friend

Your babies are crying louder
It's pounding on your brain
Your babies are crying louder now
It's pounding on your brain
Your wife's screams are stabbin' you
Like the dirty drivin' rain

Your grass it is turning black
There's no water in your well
Your grass is turning black
There's no water in your well
You spent your last lone dollar
On seven shotgun shells

Way out in the wilderness
A cold coyote calls
Way out in the wilderness
A cold coyote calls
Your eyes fix on the shotgun
That's hangin' on the wall

Your brain is a-bleedin'
And your legs can't seem to stand
Your brain is a-bleedin'
And your legs can't seem to stand
Your eyes fix on the shotgun
That you're holdin' in your hand

There's seven breezes a-blowin'
All around the cabin door
There's seven breezes a-blowin'
All around the cabin door
Seven shots ring out
Like the ocean's pounding roar

There's seven people dead

On a South Dakota farm
There's seven people dead
On a South Dakota farm
Somewhere in the distance
There's seven new people born

ONE TOO MANY MORNINGS

Down the street the dogs are barkin'
And the day is a-gettin' dark
As the night comes in a-fallin'
The dogs'll lose their bark
An' the silent night will shatter
From the sounds inside my mind
For I'm one too many mornings
And a thousand miles behind

From the crossroads of my doorstep
My eyes they start to fade
As I turn my head back to the room
Where my love and I have laid
An' I gaze back to the street
The sidewalk and the sign
And I'm one too many mornings
An' a thousand miles behind

It's a restless hungry feeling
That don't mean no one no good
When ev'rything I'm a-sayin'
You can say it just as good
You're right from your side
I'm right from mine
We're both just one too many mornings
An' a thousand miles behind

ONLY A PAWN IN THEIR GAME

A bullet from the back of a bush took Medgar Evers' blood
A finger fired the trigger to his name
A handle hid out in the dark
A hand set the spark
Two eyes took the aim
Behind a man's brain
But he can't be blamed
He's only a pawn in their game

A South politician preaches to the poor white man
"You got more than the blacks, don't complain
You're better than them, you been born with white skin," they explain
And the Negro's name
Is used it is plain
For the politician's gain
As he rises to fame
And the poor white remains
On the caboose of the train
But it ain't him to blame
He's only a pawn in their game

The deputy sheriffs, the soldiers, the governors get paid
And the marshals and cops get the same
But the poor white man's used in the hands of them all like a tool
He's taught in his school
From the start by the rule
That the laws are with him
To protect his white skin
To keep up his hate
So he never thinks straight
'Bout the shape that he's in
But it ain't him to blame
He's only a pawn in their game

From the poverty shacks, he looks from the cracks to the tracks

And the hoofbeats pound in his brain
And he's taught how to walk in a pack
Shoot in the back
With his fist in a clinch
To hang and to lynch
To hide 'neath the hood
To kill with no pain
Like a dog on a chain
He ain't got no name
But it ain't him to blame
He's only a pawn in their game

Today, Medgar Evers was buried from the bullet he caught
They lowered him down as a king
But when the shadowy sun sets on the one
That fired the gun
He'll see by his grave
On the stone that remains
Carved next to his name
His epitaph plain:
Only a pawn in their game

BOOTS OF SPANISH LEATHER

Oh, I'm sailin' away my own true love
I'm sailin' away in the morning
Is there something I can send you from across the sea
From the place that I'll be landing?

No, there's nothin' you can send me, my own true love
There's nothin' I wish to be ownin'
Just carry yourself back to me unspoiled
From across that lonesome ocean

Oh, but I just thought you might want something fine
Made of silver or of golden
Either from the mountains of Madrid
Or from the coast of Barcelona

Oh, but if I had the stars from the darkest night
And the diamonds from the deepest ocean
I'd forsake them all for your sweet kiss
For that's all I'm wishin' to be ownin'

That I might be gone a long time
And it's only that I'm askin'
Is there something I can send you to remember me by
To make your time more easy passin'

Oh, how can, how can you ask me again
It only brings me sorrow
The same thing I want from you today
I would want again tomorrow

I got a letter on a lonesome day
It was from her ship a-sailin'
Saying I don't know when I'll be comin' back again
It depends on how I'm a-feelin'

Well, if you, my love, must think that-a-way
I'm sure your mind is roamin'
I'm sure your heart is not with me
But with the country to where you're goin'

So take heed, take heed of the western wind
Take heed of the stormy weather
And yes, there's something you can send back to me
Spanish boots of Spanish leather

THE LONESOME DEATH
OF HATTIE CARROLL

William Zanzinger killed poor Hattie Carroll
With a cane that he twirled around his diamond ring finger
At a Baltimore hotel society gath'rin'
And the cops were called in and his weapon took from him
As they rode him in custody down to the station
And booked William Zanzinger for first-degree murder
But you who philosophize disgrace and criticize all fears
Take the rag away from your face
Now ain't the time for your tears

William Zanzinger, who at twenty-four years
Owns a tobacco farm of six hundred acres
With rich wealthy parents who provide and protect him
And high office relations in the politics of Maryland
Reacted to his deed with a shrug of his shoulders
And swear words and sneering, and his tongue it was snarling
In a matter of minutes on bail was out walking
But you who philosophize disgrace and criticize all fears
Take the rag away from your face
Now ain't the time for your tears

Hattie Carroll was a maid of the kitchen
She was fifty-one years old and gave birth to ten children
Who carried the dishes and took out the garbage
And never sat once at the head of the table
And didn't even talk to the people at the table
Who just cleaned up all the food from the table
And emptied the ashtrays on a whole other level
Got killed by a blow, lay slain by a cane
That sailed through the air and came down through the room
Doomed and determined to destroy all the gentle
And she never done nothing to William Zanzinger

But you who philosophize disgrace and criticize all fears
Take the rag away from your face
Now ain't the time for your tears

In the courtroom of honor, the judge pounded his gavel
To show that all's equal and that the courts are on the level
And that the strings in the books ain't pulled and persuaded
And that even the nobles get properly handled
Once that the cops have chased after and caught 'em
And that the ladder of law has no top and no bottom
Stared at the person who killed for no reason
Who just happened to be feelin' that way without warnin'
And he spoke through his cloak, most deep and distinguished
And handed out strongly, for penalty and repentance
William Zanzinger with a six-month sentence
Oh, but you who philosophize disgrace and criticize all fears
Bury the rag deep in your face
For now's the time for your tears

LAY DOWN YOUR WEARY TUNE

Lay down your weary tune, lay down
Lay down the song you strum
And rest yourself 'neath the strength of strings
No voice can hope to hum

Struck by the sounds before the sun
I knew the night had gone
The morning breeze like a bugle blew
Against the drums of dawn

Lay down your weary tune, lay down
Lay down the song you strum
And rest yourself 'neath the strength of strings
No voice can hope to hum

The ocean wild like an organ played
The seaweed's wove its strands
The crashin' waves like cymbals clashed
Against the rocks and sands

Lay down your weary tune, lay down
Lay down the song you strum
And rest yourself 'neath the strength of strings
No voice can hope to hum

I stood unwound beneath the skies
And clouds unbound by laws
The cryin' rain like a trumpet sang
And asked for no applause

Lay down your weary tune, lay down
Lay down the song you strum
And rest yourself 'neath the strength of strings
No voice can hope to hum

The last of leaves fell from the trees

And clung to a new love's breast
The branches bare like a banjo played
To the winds that listened best

I gazed down in the river's mirror
And watched its winding strum
The water smooth ran like a hymn
And like a harp did hum

Lay down your weary tune, lay down
Lay down the song you strum
And rest yourself 'neath the strength of strings
No voice can hope to hum

CHIMES OF FREEDOM

Far between sundown's finish an' midnight's broken toll
We ducked inside the doorway, thunder crashing
As majestic bells of bolts struck shadows in the sounds
Seeming to be the chimes of freedom flashing
Flashing for the warriors whose strength is not to fight
Flashing for the refugees on the unarmed road of flight
An' for each an' ev'ry underdog soldier in the night
An' we gazed upon the chimes of freedom flashing

In the city's melted furnace, unexpectedly we watched
With faces hidden while the walls were tightening
As the echo of the wedding bells before the blowin' rain
Dissolved into the bells of the lightning
Tolling for the rebel, tolling for the rake
Tolling for the luckless, the abandoned an' forsaked
Tolling for the outcast, burnin' constantly at stake
An' we gazed upon the chimes of freedom flashing

Through the mad mystic hammering of the wild ripping hail
The sky cracked its poems in naked wonder
That the clinging of the church bells blew far into the breeze
Leaving only bells of lightning and its thunder
Striking for the gentle, striking for the kind
Striking for the guardians and protectors of the mind
An' the unpawned painter behind beyond his rightful time
An' we gazed upon the chimes of freedom flashing

Through the wild cathedral evening the rain unraveled tales
For the disrobed faceless forms of no position
Tolling for the tongues with no place to bring their thoughts
All down in taken-for-granted situations
Tolling for the deaf an' blind, tolling for the mute
Tolling for the mistreated, mateless mother, the mistitled prostitute
For the misdemeanor outlaw, chased an' cheated by pursuit
An' we gazed upon the chimes of freedom flashing

Even though a cloud's white curtain in a far-off corner flashed
An' the hypnotic splattered mist was slowly lifting
Electric light still struck like arrows, fired but for the ones
Condemned to drift or else be kept from drifting
Tolling for the searching ones, on their speechless, seeking trail
For the lonesome-hearted lovers with too personal a tale
An' for each unharmful, gentle soul misplaced inside a jail
An' we gazed upon the chimes of freedom flashing

Starry-eyed an' laughing as I recall when we were caught
Trapped by no track of hours for they hanged suspended
As we listened one last time an' we watched with one last look
Spellbound an' swallowed 'til the tolling ended
Tolling for the aching ones whose wounds cannot be nursed
For the countless confused, accused, misused, strung-out ones an' worse
An' for every hung-up person in the whole wide universe
An' we gazed upon the chimes of freedom flashing

MOTORPSYCHO NIGHTMARE

I pounded on a farmhouse
Lookin' for a place to stay
I was mighty, mighty tired
I had come a long, long way
I said, "Hey, hey, in there
Is there anybody home?"
I was standin' on the steps
Feelin' most alone
Well, out comes a farmer
He must have thought that I was nuts
He immediately looked at me
And stuck a gun into my guts

I fell down
To my bended knees
Saying, "I dig farmers
Don't shoot me, please!"
He cocked his rifle
And began to shout
"You're that travelin' salesman
That I have heard about"

I said, "No! No! No!
I'm a doctor and it's true
I'm a clean-cut kid
And I been to college, too"

Then in comes his daughter
Whose name was Rita
She looked like she stepped out of
La Dolce Vita
I immediately tried to cool it
With her dad
And told him what a
Nice, pretty farm he had
He said, "What do doctors
Know about farms, pray tell?"
I said, "I was born
At the bottom of a wishing well"

Well, by the dirt 'neath my nails
I guess he knew I wouldn't lie
"I guess you're tired"
He said, kinda sly
I said, "Yes, ten thousand miles
Today I drove"
He said, "I got a bed for you
Underneath the stove

Just one condition
And you go to sleep right now
That you don't touch my daughter
And in the morning, milk the cow"

I was sleepin' like a rat
When I heard something jerkin'
There stood Rita
Lookin' just like Tony Perkins
She said, "Would you like to take a shower?
I'll show you up to the door"
I said, "Oh, no! no!
I've been through this before"
I knew I had to split
But I didn't know how
When she said
"Would you like to take that shower, now?"

Well, I couldn't leave
Unless the old man chased me out
'Cause I'd already promised
That I'd milk his cows
I had to say something
To strike him very weird
So I yelled out
"I like Fidel Castro and his beard"
Rita looked offended
But she got out of the way
As he came charging down the stairs
Sayin', "What's that I heard you say?"

I said, "I like Fidel Castro
I think you heard me right"
And ducked as he swung
At me with all his might
Rita mumbled something

'Bout her mother on the hill
As his fist hit the icebox
He said he's going to kill me
If I don't get out the door
In two seconds flat
"You unpatriotic
Rotten doctor Commie rat"

Well, he threw a *Reader's Digest*
At my head and I did run
I did a somersault
As I seen him get his gun
And crashed through the window
At a hundred miles an hour
And landed fully blast
In his garden flowers
Rita said, "Come back!"
As he started to load
The sun was comin' up
And I was runnin' down the road

Well, I don't figure I'll be back
There for a spell
Even though Rita moved away
And got a job in a motel
He still waits for me
Constant, on the sly
He wants to turn me in
To the F.B.I.
Me, I romp and stomp
Thankful as I romp
Without freedom of speech
I might be in the swamp

MY BACK PAGES

Crimson flames tied through my ears
Rollin' high and mighty traps
Pounced with fire on flaming roads
Using ideas as my maps
"We'll meet on edges, soon," said I
Proud 'neath heated brow
Ah, but I was so much older then
I'm younger than that now

Half-wracked prejudice leaped forth
"Rip down all hate," I screamed
Lies that life is black and white
Spoke from my skull. I dreamed
Romantic facts of musketeers
Foundationed deep, somehow
Ah, but I was so much older then
I'm younger than that now

Girls' faces formed the forward path
From phony jealousy
To memorizing politics
Of ancient history
Flung down by corpse evangelists
Unthought of, though, somehow
Ah, but I was so much older then
I'm younger than that now

A self-ordained professor's tongue
Too serious to fool
Spouted out that liberty
Is just equality in school

"Equality," I spoke the word
As if a wedding vow
Ah, but I was so much older then
I'm younger than that now

In a soldier's stance, I aimed my hand
At the mongrel dogs who teach
Fearing not that I'd become my enemy
In the instant that I preach
My pathway led by confusion boats
Mutiny from stern to bow
Ah, but I was so much older then
I'm younger than that now

Yes, my guard stood hard when abstract threats
Too noble to neglect
Deceived me into thinking
I had something to protect
Good and bad, I define these terms
Quite clear, no doubt, somehow
Ah, but I was so much older then
I'm younger than that now

IT AIN'T ME, BABE

Go 'way from my window
Leave at your own chosen speed
I'm not the one you want, babe
I'm not the one you need
You say you're lookin' for someone
Never weak but always strong
To protect you an' defend you
Whether you are right or wrong
Someone to open each and every door
But it ain't me, babe
No, no, no, it ain't me, babe
It ain't me you're lookin' for, babe

Go lightly from the ledge, babe
Go lightly on the ground
I'm not the one you want, babe
I will only let you down
You say you're lookin' for someone
Who will promise never to part
Someone to close his eyes for you
Someone to close his heart
Someone who will die for you an' more
But it ain't me, babe
No, no, no, it ain't me, babe
It ain't me you're lookin' for, babe

Go melt back into the night, babe
Everything inside is made of stone
There's nothing in here moving
An' anyway I'm not alone
You say you're looking for someone

Who'll pick you up each time you fall
To gather flowers constantly
An' to come each time you call
A lover for your life an' nothing more
But it ain't me, babe
No, no, no, it ain't me, babe
It ain't me you're lookin' for, babe

SUBTERRANEAN HOMESICK BLUES

Johnny's in the basement
Mixing up the medicine
I'm on the pavement
Thinking about the government
The man in the trench coat
Badge out, laid off
Says he's got a bad cough
Wants to get it paid off
Look out kid
It's somethin' you did
God knows when
But you're doin' it again
You better duck down the alley way
Lookin' for a new friend
The man in the coon-skin cap
In the big pen
Wants eleven dollar bills
You only got ten

Maggie comes fleet foot
Face full of black soot
Talkin' that the heat put
Plants in the bed but
The phone's tapped anyway
Maggie says that many say
They must bust in early May
Orders from the D.A.
Look out kid
Don't matter what you did
Walk on your tiptoes
Don't try "No-Doz"
Better stay away from those
That carry around a fire hose
Keep a clean nose
Watch the plain clothes
You don't need a weatherman
To know which way the wind blows

Get sick, get well
Hang around a ink well
Ring bell, hard to tell
If anything is goin' to sell
Try hard, get barred
Get back, write braille
Get jailed, jump bail
Join the army, if you fail
Look out kid
You're gonna get hit
But users, cheaters
Six-time losers
Hang around the theaters
Girl by the whirlpool
Lookin' for a new fool
Don't follow leaders
Watch the parkin' meters

Ah get born, keep warm
Short pants, romance, learn to dance
Get dressed, get blessed
Try to be a success
Please her, please him, buy gifts
Don't steal, don't lift
Twenty years of schoolin'
And they put you on the day shift
Look out kid
They keep it all hid
Better jump down a manhole
Light yourself a candle
Don't wear sandals
Try to avoid the scandals
Don't wanna be a bum
You better chew gum
The pump don't work
'Cause the vandals took the handles

LOVE MINUS ZERO/NO LIMIT

My love she speaks like silence
Without ideals or violence
She doesn't have to say she's faithful
Yet she's true, like ice, like fire
People carry roses
Make promises by the hours
My love she laughs like the flowers
Valentines can't buy her

In the dime stores and bus stations
People talk of situations
Read books, repeat quotations
Draw conclusions on the wall
Some speak of the future
My love she speaks softly
She knows there's no success like failure
And that failure's no success at all

The cloak and dagger dangles
Madams light the candles
In ceremonies of the horsemen
Even the pawn must hold a grudge
Statues made of matchsticks
Crumble into one another
My love winks, she does not bother
She knows too much to argue or to judge

The bridge at midnight trembles
The country doctor rambles
Bankers' nieces seek perfection
Expecting all the gifts that wise men bring
The wind howls like a hammer
The night blows cold and rainy
My love she's like some raven
At my window with a broken wing

MR. TAMBOURINE MAN

Hey! Mr. Tambourine Man, play a song for me
I'm not sleepy and there is no place I'm going to
Hey! Mr. Tambourine Man, play a song for me
In the jingle jangle morning I'll come followin' you

Though I know that evenin's empire has returned into sand
Vanished from my hand
Left me blindly here to stand but still not sleeping
My weariness amazes me, I'm branded on my feet
I have no one to meet
And the ancient empty street's too dead for dreaming

Hey! Mr. Tambourine Man, play a song for me
I'm not sleepy and there is no place I'm going to
Hey! Mr. Tambourine Man, play a song for me
In the jingle jangle morning I'll come followin' you

Take me on a trip upon your magic swirlin' ship
My senses have been stripped, my hands can't feel to grip
My toes too numb to step
Wait only for my boot heels to be wanderin'
I'm ready to go anywhere, I'm ready for to fade
Into my own parade, cast your dancing spell my way
I promise to go under it

Hey! Mr. Tambourine Man, play a song for me
I'm not sleepy and there is no place I'm going to
Hey! Mr. Tambourine Man, play a song for me
In the jingle jangle morning I'll come followin' you

Though you might hear laughin', spinnin', swingin' madly across the sun
It's not aimed at anyone, it's just escapin' on the run
And but for the sky there are no fences facin'
And if you hear vague traces of skippin' reels of rhyme
To your tambourine in time, it's just a ragged clown behind
I wouldn't pay it any mind
It's just a shadow you're seein' that he's chasing

Hey! Mr. Tambourine Man, play a song for me
I'm not sleepy and there is no place I'm going to
Hey! Mr. Tambourine Man, play a song for me
In the jingle jangle morning I'll come followin' you

Then take me disappearin' through the smoke rings of my mind
Down the foggy ruins of time, far past the frozen leaves
The haunted, frightened trees, out to the windy beach
Far from the twisted reach of crazy sorrow
Yes, to dance beneath the diamond sky with one hand waving free
Silhouetted by the sea, circled by the circus sands
With all memory and fate driven deep beneath the waves
Let me forget about today until tomorrow

Hey! Mr. Tambourine Man, play a song for me
I'm not sleepy and there is no place I'm going to
Hey! Mr. Tambourine Man, play a song for me
In the jingle jangle morning I'll come followin' you

BOB DYLAN'S 115TH DREAM

I was riding on the Mayflower
When I thought I spied some land
I yelled for Captain Arab
I have yuh understand
Who came running to the deck
Said, "Boys, forget the whale
Look on over yonder
Cut the engines
Change the sail
Haul on the bowline"
We sang that melody
Like all tough sailors do
When they are far away at sea

"I think I'll call it America"
I said as we hit land
I took a deep breath
I fell down, I could not stand
Captain Arab he started
Writing up some deeds
He said, "Let's set up a fort
And start buying the place with beads"
Just then this cop comes down the street
Crazy as a loon
He throw us all in jail
For carryin' harpoons

Ah me I busted out
Don't even ask me how
I went to get some help
I walked by a Guernsey cow
Who directed me down
To the Bowery slums
Where people carried signs around
Saying, "Ban the bums"
I jumped right into line
Sayin', "I hope that I'm not late"
When I realized I hadn't eaten
For five days straight

I went into a restaurant
Lookin' for the cook
I told them I was the editor
Of a famous etiquette book
The waitress he was handsome
He wore a powder blue cape
I ordered some suzette, I said
"Could you please make that crepe"
Just then the whole kitchen exploded
From boilin' fat
Food was flying everywhere
And I left without my hat

Now, I didn't mean to be nosy
But I went into a bank
To get some bail for Arab
And all the boys back in the tank
They asked me for some collateral
And I pulled down my pants
They threw me in the alley
When up comes this girl from France
Who invited me to her house
I went, but she had a friend
Who knocked me out
And robbed my boots
And I was on the street again

Well, I rapped upon a house
With the U.S. flag upon display
I said, "Could you help me out
I got some friends down the way"
The man says, "Get out of here
I'll tear you limb from limb"
I said, "You know they refused Jesus, too"
He said, "You're not Him
Get out of here before I break your bones
I ain't your pop"
I decided to have him arrested
And I went looking for a cop

I ran right outside
And I hopped inside a cab
I went out the other door
This Englishman said, "Fab"
As he saw me leap a hot dog stand
And a chariot that stood
Parked across from a building
Advertising brotherhood
I ran right through the front door
Like a hobo sailor does
But it was just a funeral parlor
And the man asked me who I was

I repeated that my friends
Were all in jail, with a sigh
He gave me his card
He said, "Call me if they die"
I shook his hand and said goodbye
Ran out to the street
When a bowling ball came down the road
And knocked me off my feet
A pay phone was ringing
It just about blew my mind
When I picked it up and said hello
This foot came through the line

Well, by this time I was fed up
At tryin' to make a stab
At bringin' back any help
For my friends and Captain Arab
I decided to flip a coin
Like either heads or tails
Would let me know if I should go
Back to ship or back to jail
So I hocked my sailor suit
And I got a coin to flip
It came up tails
It rhymed with sails
So I made it back to the ship

Well, I got back and took
The parkin' ticket off the mast
I was ripping it to shreds
When this coastguard boat went past
They asked me my name
And I said, "Captain Kidd"
They believed me but
They wanted to know
What exactly that I did
I said for the Pope of Eruke
I was employed
They let me go right away
They were very paranoid

Well, the last I heard of Arab
He was stuck on a whale
That was married to the deputy
Sheriff of the jail
But the funniest thing was
When I was leavin' the bay
I saw three ships a-sailin'
They were all heading my way
I asked the captain what his name was
And how come he didn't drive a truck
He said his name was Columbus
I just said, "Good luck"

GATES OF EDEN

Of war and peace the truth just twists
Its curfew gull just glides
Upon four-legged forest clouds
The cowboy angel rides
With his candle lit into the sun
Though its glow is waxed in black
All except when 'neath the trees of Eden

The lamppost stands with folded arms
Its iron claws attached
To curbs 'neath holes where babies wail
Though it shadows metal badge
All and all can only fall
With a crashing but meaningless blow
No sound ever comes from the Gates of Eden

The savage soldier sticks his head in sand
And then complains
Unto the shoeless hunter who's gone deaf
But still remains
Upon the beach where hound dogs bay
At ships with tattooed sails
Heading for the Gates of Eden

With a time-rusted compass blade
Aladdin and his lamp
Sits with Utopian hermit monks
Sidesaddle on the Golden Calf
And on their promises of paradise
You will not hear a laugh
All except inside the Gates of Eden

Relationships of ownership
They whisper in the wings
To those condemned to act accordingly
And wait for succeeding kings
And I try to harmonize with songs
The lonesome sparrow sings
There are no kings inside the Gates of Eden

The motorcycle black madonna
Two-wheeled gypsy queen
And her silver-studded phantom cause
The gray flannel dwarf to scream
As he weeps to wicked birds of prey
Who pick up on his bread crumb sins
And there are no sins inside the Gates of Eden

The kingdoms of Experience
In the precious wind they rot
While paupers change possessions
Each one wishing for what the other has got
And the princess and the prince
Discuss what's real and what is not
It doesn't matter inside the Gates of Eden

The foreign sun, it squints upon
A bed that is never mine
As friends and other strangers
From their fates try to resign
Leaving men wholly, totally free
To do anything they wish to do but die
And there are no trials inside the Gates of Eden

At dawn my lover comes to me
And tells me of her dreams
With no attempts to shovel the glimpse
Into the ditch of what each one means
At times I think there are no words
But these to tell what's true
And there are no truths outside the Gates of Eden

IT'S ALRIGHT, MA
(I'M ONLY BLEEDING)

Darkness at the break of noon
Shadows even the silver spoon
The handmade blade, the child's balloon
Eclipses both the sun and moon
To understand you know too soon
There is no sense in trying

Pointed threats, they bluff with scorn
Suicide remarks are torn
From the fool's gold mouthpiece the hollow horn
Plays wasted words, proves to warn
That he not busy being born is busy dying

Temptation's page flies out the door
You follow, find yourself at war
Watch waterfalls of pity roar
You feel to moan but unlike before
You discover that you'd just be one more
Person crying

So don't fear if you hear
A foreign sound to your ear
It's alright, Ma, I'm only sighing

As some warn victory, some downfall
Private reasons great or small
Can be seen in the eyes of those that call
To make all that should be killed to crawl
While others say don't hate nothing at all
Except hatred

Disillusioned words like bullets bark
As human gods aim for their mark
Make everything from toy guns that spark
To flesh-colored Christs that glow in the dark
It's easy to see without looking too far
That not much is really sacred

While preachers preach of evil fates
Teachers teach that knowledge waits
Can lead to hundred-dollar plates
Goodness hides behind its gates
But even the president of the United States
Sometimes must have to stand naked

An' though the rules of the road have been lodged
It's only people's games that you got to dodge
And it's alright, Ma, I can make it

Advertising signs they con
You into thinking you're the one
That can do what's never been done
That can win what's never been won
Meantime life outside goes on
All around you

You lose yourself, you reappear
You suddenly find you got nothing to fear
Alone you stand with nobody near
When a trembling distant voice, unclear
Startles your sleeping ears to hear
That somebody thinks they really found you

A question in your nerves is lit
Yet you know there is no answer fit
To satisfy, insure you not to quit
To keep it in your mind and not forget
That it is not he or she or them or it
That you belong to

Although the masters make the rules
For the wise men and the fools
I got nothing, Ma, to live up to

For them that must obey authority
That they do not respect in any degree
Who despise their jobs, their destinies
Speak jealously of them that are free
Cultivate their flowers to be
Nothing more than something they invest in

While some on principles baptized
To strict party platform ties
Social clubs in drag disguise
Outsiders they can freely criticize
Tell nothing except who to idolize
And then say God bless him

While one who sings with his tongue on fire
Gargles in the rat race choir
Bent out of shape from society's pliers
Cares not to come up any higher
But rather get you down in the hole
That he's in

But I mean no harm nor put fault
On anyone that lives in a vault
But it's alright, Ma, if I can't please him

Old lady judges watch people in pairs
Limited in sex, they dare
To push fake morals, insult and stare
While money doesn't talk, it swears
Obscenity, who really cares
Propaganda, all is phony

While them that defend what they cannot see
With a killer's pride, security
It blows the minds most bitterly
For them that think death's honesty
Won't fall upon them naturally
Life sometimes must get lonely

My eyes collide head-on with stuffed
Graveyards, false gods, I scuff
At pettiness which plays so rough
Walk upside-down inside handcuffs
Kick my legs to crash it off
Say okay, I have had enough
What else can you show me?

And if my thought-dreams could be seen
They'd probably put my head in a guillotine
But it's alright, Ma, it's life, and life only

IT'S ALL OVER NOW, BABY BLUE

You must leave now, take what you need, you think will last
But whatever you wish to keep, you better grab it fast
Yonder stands your orphan with his gun
Crying like a fire in the sun
Look out the saints are comin' through
And it's all over now, Baby Blue

The highway is for gamblers, better use your sense
Take what you have gathered from coincidence
The empty-handed painter from your streets
Is drawing crazy patterns on your sheets
This sky, too, is folding under you
And it's all over now, Baby Blue

All your seasick sailors, they are rowing home
All your reindeer armies, are all going home
The lover who just walked out your door
Has taken all his blankets from the floor
The carpet, too, is moving under you
And it's all over now, Baby Blue

Leave your stepping stones behind, something calls for you
Forget the dead you've left, they will not follow you
The vagabond who's rapping at your door
Is standing in the clothes that you once wore
Strike another match, go start anew
And it's all over now, Baby Blue

LIKE A ROLLING STONE

Once upon a time you dressed so fine
You threw the bums a dime in your prime, didn't you?
People'd call, say, "Beware doll, you're bound to fall"
You thought they were all kiddin' you
You used to laugh about
Everybody that was hangin' out
Now you don't talk so loud
Now you don't seem so proud
About having to be scrounging for your next meal

How does it feel
How does it feel
To be without a home
Like a complete unknown
Like a rolling stone?

You've gone to the finest school all right, Miss Lonely
But you know you only used to get juiced in it
And nobody has ever taught you how to live on the street
And now you find out you're gonna have to get used to it
You said you'd never compromise
With the mystery tramp, but now you realize
He's not selling any alibis
As you stare into the vacuum of his eyes
And ask him do you want to make a deal?

How does it feel
How does it feel
To be on your own
With no direction home
Like a complete unknown
Like a rolling stone?

You never turned around to see the frowns on the jugglers and the clowns
When they all come down and did tricks for you
You never understood that it ain't no good
You shouldn't let other people get your kicks for you
You used to ride on the chrome horse with your diplomat
Who carried on his shoulder a Siamese cat
Ain't it hard when you discover that
He really wasn't where it's at
After he took from you everything he could steal

How does it feel
How does it feel
To be on your own
With no direction home
Like a complete unknown
Like a rolling stone?

Princess on the steeple and all the pretty people
They're drinkin', thinkin' that they got it made
Exchanging all kinds of precious gifts and things
But you'd better lift your diamond ring, you'd better pawn it babe
You used to be so amused
At Napoleon in rags and the language that he used
Go to him now, he calls you, you can't refuse
When you got nothing, you got nothing to lose
You're invisible now, you got no secrets to conceal

How does it feel
How does it feel
To be on your own
With no direction home
Like a complete unknown
Like a rolling stone?

TOMBSTONE BLUES

The sweet pretty things are in bed now of course
The city fathers they're trying to endorse
The reincarnation of Paul Revere's horse
But the town has no need to be nervous

The ghost of Belle Starr she hands down her wits
To Jezebel the nun she violently knits
A bald wig for Jack the Ripper who sits
At the head of the chamber of commerce

Mama's in the fact'ry
She ain't got no shoes
Daddy's in the alley
He's lookin' for the fuse
I'm in the streets
With the tombstone blues

The hysterical bride in the penny arcade
Screaming she moans, "I've just been made"
Then sends out for the doctor who pulls down the shade
Says, "My advice is to not let the boys in"

Now the medicine man comes and he shuffles inside
He walks with a swagger and he says to the bride
"Stop all this weeping, swallow your pride
You will not die, it's not poison"

Mama's in the fact'ry
She ain't got no shoes
Daddy's in the alley
He's lookin' for the fuse
I'm in the streets
With the tombstone blues

Well, John the Baptist after torturing a thief
Looks up at his hero the Commander-in-Chief
Saying, "Tell me great hero, but please make it brief
Is there a hole for me to get sick in?"

The Commander-in-Chief answers him while chasing a fly
Saying, "Death to all those who would whimper and cry"
And dropping a barbell he points to the sky
Saying, "The sun's not yellow it's chicken"

Mama's in the fact'ry
She ain't got no shoes
Daddy's in the alley
He's lookin' for the fuse
I'm in the streets
With the tombstone blues

The king of the Philistines his soldiers to save
Puts jawbones on their tombstones and flatters their graves
Puts the pied pipers in prison and fattens the slaves
Then sends them out to the jungle

Gypsy Davey with a blowtorch he burns out their camps
With his faithful slave Pedro behind him he tramps
With a fantastic collection of stamps
To win friends and influence his uncle

Mama's in the fact'ry
She ain't got no shoes
Daddy's in the alley
He's lookin' for the fuse
I'm in the streets
With the tombstone blues

The geometry of innocence flesh on the bone
Causes Galileo's math book to get thrown
At Delilah who sits worthlessly alone
But the tears on her cheeks are from laughter

Now I wish I could give Brother Bill his great thrill
I would set him in chains at the top of the hill
Then send out for some pillars and Cecil B. DeMille
He could die happily ever after

Mama's in the fact'ry
She ain't got no shoes
Daddy's in the alley
He's lookin' for the fuse
I'm in the streets
With the tombstone blues

Where Ma Rainey and Beethoven once unwrapped their bedroll
Tuba players now rehearse around the flagpole
And the National Bank at a profit sells road maps for the soul
To the old folks home and the college

Now I wish I could write you a melody so plain
That could hold you dear lady from going insane
That could ease you and cool you and cease the pain
Of your useless and pointless knowledge

Mama's in the fact'ry
She ain't got no shoes
Daddy's in the alley
He's lookin' for the fuse
I'm in the streets
With the tombstone blues

BALLAD OF A THIN MAN

You walk into the room
With your pencil in your hand
You see somebody naked
And you say, "Who is that man?"
You try so hard
But you don't understand
Just what you'll say
When you get home

Because something is happening here
But you don't know what it is
Do you, Mister Jones?

You raise up your head
And you ask, "Is this where it is?"
And somebody points to you and says
"It's his"
And you say, "What's mine?"
And somebody else says, "Where what is?"
And you say, "Oh my God
Am I here all alone?"

Because something is happening here
But you don't know what it is
Do you, Mister Jones?

You hand in your ticket
And you go watch the geek
Who immediately walks up to you
When he hears you speak
And says, "How does it feel
To be such a freak?"
And you say, "Impossible"
As he hands you a bone

Because something is happening here
But you don't know what it is
Do you, Mister Jones?

You have many contacts
Among the lumberjacks
To get you facts
When someone attacks your imagination
But nobody has any respect
Anyway they already expect you
To just give a check
To tax-deductible charity organizations

You've been with the professors
And they've all liked your looks
With great lawyers you have
Discussed lepers and crooks
You've been through all of
F. Scott Fitzgerald's books
You're very well read
It's well known

Because something is happening here
But you don't know what it is
Do you, Mister Jones?

Well, the sword swallower, he comes up to you
And then he kneels
He crosses himself
And then he clicks his high heels
And without further notice
He asks you how it feels
And he says, "Here is your throat back
Thanks for the loan"

Because something is happening here
But you don't know what it is
Do you, Mister Jones?

Now you see this one-eyed midget
Shouting the word "NOW"
And you say, "For what reason?"
And he says, "How?"
And you say, "What does this mean?"
And he screams back, "You're a cow
Give me some milk
Or else go home"

Because something is happening here
But you don't know what it is
Do you, Mister Jones?

Well, you walk into the room
Like a camel and then you frown
You put your eyes in your pocket
And your nose on the ground
There ought to be a law
Against you comin' around
You should be made
To wear earphones

Because something is happening here
But you don't know what it is
Do you, Mister Jones?

HIGHWAY 61 REVISITED

Oh God said to Abraham, "Kill me a son"
Abe says, "Man, you must be puttin' me on"
God say, "No." Abe say, "What?"
God say, "You can do what you want Abe, but
The next time you see me comin' you better run"
Well Abe says, "Where do you want this killin' done?"
God says, "Out on Highway 61"

Well Georgia Sam he had a bloody nose
Welfare Department they wouldn't give him no clothes
He asked poor Howard where can I go
Howard said there's only one place I know
Sam said tell me quick man I got to run
Ol' Howard just pointed with his gun
And said that way down on Highway 61

Well Mack the Finger said to Louie the King
I got forty red white and blue shoestrings
And a thousand telephones that don't ring
Do you know where I can get rid of these things
And Louie the King said let me think for a minute son
And he said yes I think it can be easily done
Just take everything down to Highway 61

Now the fifth daughter on the twelfth night
Told the first father that things weren't right
My complexion she said is much too white
He said come here and step into the light he says hmm you're right
Let me tell the second mother this has been done
But the second mother was with the seventh son
And they were both out on Highway 61

Now the rovin' gambler he was very bored
He was tryin' to create a next world war
He found a promoter who nearly fell off the floor
He said I never engaged in this kind of thing before
But yes I think it can be very easily done
We'll just put some bleachers out in the sun
And have it on Highway 61

JUST LIKE TOM THUMB'S BLUES

When you're lost in the rain in Juarez
And it's Eastertime too
And your gravity fails
And negativity don't pull you through
Don't put on any airs
When you're down on Rue Morgue Avenue
They got some hungry women there
And they really make a mess outa you

Now if you see Saint Annie
Please tell her thanks a lot
I cannot move
My fingers are all in a knot
I don't have the strength
To get up and take another shot
And my best friend, my doctor
Won't even say what it is I've got

Sweet Melinda
The peasants call her the goddess of gloom
She speaks good English
And she invites you up into her room
And you're so kind
And careful not to go to her too soon
And she takes your voice
And leaves you howling at the moon

Up on Housing Project Hill
It's either fortune or fame
You must pick up one or the other
Though neither of them are to be what they claim
If you're lookin' to get silly
You better go back to from where you came
Because the cops don't need you
And man they expect the same

Now all the authorities
They just stand around and boast
How they blackmailed the sergeant-at-arms
Into leaving his post
And picking up Angel who
Just arrived here from the coast
Who looked so fine at first
But left looking just like a ghost

I started out on burgundy
But soon hit the harder stuff
Everybody said they'd stand behind me
When the game got rough
But the joke was on me
There was nobody even there to call my bluff
I'm going back to New York City
I do believe I've had enough

Praise be to Nero's Neptune
The Titanic sails at dawn
And everybody's shouting
"Which Side Are You On?"
And Ezra Pound and T. S. Eliot
Fighting in the captain's tower
While calypso singers laugh at them
And fishermen hold flowers
Between the windows of the sea
Where lovely mermaids flow
And nobody has to think too much
About Desolation Row

Yes, I received your letter yesterday
(About the time the doorknob broke)
When you asked how I was doing
Was that some kind of joke?
All these people that you mention
Yes, I know them, they're quite lame
I had to rearrange their faces
And give them all another name
Right now I can't read too good
Don't send me no more letters no
Not unless you mail them
From Desolation Row

POSITIVELY 4TH STREET

You got a lotta nerve
To say you are my friend
When I was down
You just stood there grinning

You got a lotta nerve
To say you got a helping hand to lend
You just want to be on
The side that's winning

You say I let you down
You know it's not like that
If you're so hurt
Why then don't you show it

You say you lost your faith
But that's not where it's at
You had no faith to lose
And you know it

I know the reason
That you talk behind my back
I used to be among the crowd
You're in with

Do you take me for such a fool
To think I'd make contact
With the one who tries to hide
What he don't know to begin with

You see me on the street
You always act surprised
You say, "How are you?" "Good luck"
But you don't mean it

When you know as well as me
You'd rather see me paralyzed
Why don't you just come out once
And scream it

No, I do not feel that good
When I see the heartbreaks you embrace
If I was a master thief
Perhaps I'd rob them

And now I know you're dissatisfied
With your position and your place
Don't you understand
It's not my problem

I wish that for just one time
You could stand inside my shoes
And just for that one moment
I could be you

Yes, I wish that for just one time
You could stand inside my shoes
You'd know what a drag it is
To see you

VISIONS OF JOHANNA

Ain't it just like the night to play tricks when you're trying to be so quiet?
We sit here stranded, though we're all doin' our best to deny it
And Louise holds a handful of rain, temptin' you to defy it
Lights flicker from the opposite loft
In this room the heat pipes just cough
The country music station plays soft
But there's nothing, really nothing to turn off
Just Louise and her lover so entwined
And these visions of Johanna that conquer my mind

In the empty lot where the ladies play blindman's bluff with the key chain
And the all-night girls they whisper of escapades out on the "D" train
We can hear the night watchman click his flashlight
Ask himself if it's him or them that's really insane
Louise, she's all right, she's just near
She's delicate and seems like the mirror
But she just makes it all too concise and too clear
That Johanna's not here
The ghost of 'lectricity howls in the bones of her face
Where these visions of Johanna have now taken my place

Now, little boy lost, he takes himself so seriously
He brags of his misery, he likes to live dangerously
And when bringing her name up
He speaks of a farewell kiss to me
He's sure got a lotta gall to be so useless and all
Muttering small talk at the wall while I'm in the hall
How can I explain?
Oh, it's so hard to get on
And these visions of Johanna, they kept me up past the dawn

Inside the museums, Infinity goes up on trial
Voices echo this is what salvation must be like after a while
But Mona Lisa musta had the highway blues
You can tell by the way she smiles
See the primitive wallflower freeze
When the jelly-faced women all sneeze
Hear the one with the mustache say, "Jeeze
I can't find my knees"
Oh, jewels and binoculars hang from the head of the mule
But these visions of Johanna, they make it all seem so cruel

The peddler now speaks to the countess who's pretending to care for him
Sayin', "Name me someone that's not a parasite and I'll go out and say a prayer for him"
But like Louise always says
"Ya can't look at much, can ya man?"
As she, herself, prepares for him
And Madonna, she still has not showed
We see this empty cage now corrode
Where her cape of the stage once had flowed
The fiddler, he now steps to the road
He writes ev'rything's been returned which was owed
On the back of the fish truck that loads
While my conscience explodes
The harmonicas play the skeleton keys and the rain
And these visions of Johanna are now all that remain

I WANT YOU

The guilty undertaker sighs
The lonesome organ grinder cries
The silver saxophones say I should refuse you
The cracked bells and washed-out horns
Blow into my face with scorn
But it's not that way
I wasn't born to lose you

I want you, I want you
I want you so bad
Honey, I want you

The drunken politician leaps
Upon the street where mothers weep
And the saviors who are fast asleep, they wait for you
And I wait for them to interrupt
Me drinkin' from my broken cup
And ask me to
Open up the gate for you

I want you, I want you
I want you so bad
Honey, I want you

How all my fathers, they've gone down
True love they've been without it
But all their daughters put me down
'Cause I don't think about it

Well, I return to the Queen of Spades
And talk with my chambermaid
She knows that I'm not afraid to look at her
She is good to me
And there's nothing she doesn't see
She knows where I'd like to be
But it doesn't matter

I want you, I want you
I want you so bad
Honey, I want you

Now your dancing child with his Chinese suit
He spoke to me, I took his flute
No, I wasn't very cute to him, was I?
But I did it, though, because he lied
Because he took you for a ride
And because time was on his side
And because I . . .

I want you, I want you
I want you so bad
Honey, I want you

STUCK INSIDE OF MOBILE WITH THE MEMPHIS BLUES AGAIN

Oh, the ragman draws circles
Up and down the block
I'd ask him what the matter was
But I know that he don't talk
And the ladies treat me kindly
And furnish me with tape
But deep inside my heart
I know I can't escape
Oh, Mama, can this really be the end
To be stuck inside of Mobile
With the Memphis blues again

Well, Shakespeare, he's in the alley
With his pointed shoes and his bells
Speaking to some French girl
Who says she knows me well
And I would send a message
To find out if she's talked
But the post office has been stolen
And the mailbox is locked
Oh, Mama, can this really be the end
To be stuck inside of Mobile
With the Memphis blues again

Mona tried to tell me
To stay away from the train line
She said that all the railroad men
Just drink up your blood like wine
An' I said, "Oh, I didn't know that
But then again, there's only one I've met
An' he just smoked my eyelids
An' punched my cigarette"
Oh, Mama, can this really be the end
To be stuck inside of Mobile
With the Memphis blues again

Grandpa died last week
And now he's buried in the rocks
But everybody still talks about
How badly they were shocked
But me, I expected it to happen
I knew he'd lost control
When he built a fire on Main Street
And shot it full of holes
Oh, Mama, can this really be the end
To be stuck inside of Mobile
With the Memphis blues again

Now the senator came down here
Showing ev'ryone his gun
Handing out free tickets
To the wedding of his son
An' me, I nearly got busted
An' wouldn't it be my luck
To get caught without a ticket
And be discovered beneath a truck
Oh, Mama, can this really be the end
To be stuck inside of Mobile
With the Memphis blues again

Now the preacher looked so baffled
When I asked him why he dressed
With twenty pounds of headlines
Stapled to his chest
But he cursed me when I proved it to him
Then I whispered, "Not even you can hide
You see, you're just like me
I hope you're satisfied"
Oh, Mama, can this really be the end
To be stuck inside of Mobile
With the Memphis blues again

Now the rainman gave me two cures
Then he said, "Jump right in"
The one was Texas medicine
The other was just railroad gin
An' like a fool I mixed them
An' it strangled up my mind
An' now people just get uglier
An' I have no sense of time
Oh, Mama, can this really be the end
To be stuck inside of Mobile
With the Memphis blues again

When Ruthie says come see her
In her honky-tonk lagoon
Where I can watch her waltz for free
'Neath her Panamanian moon
An' I say, "Aw come on now
You must know about my debutante"
An' she says, "Your debutante just knows what you need
But I know what you want"
Oh, Mama, can this really be the end
To be stuck inside of Mobile
With the Memphis blues again

Now the bricks lay on Grand Street
Where the neon madmen climb
They all fall there so perfectly
It all seems so well timed
An' here I sit so patiently
Waiting to find out what price
You have to pay to get out of
Going through all these things twice
Oh, Mama, can this really be the end
To be stuck inside of Mobile
With the Memphis blues again

JUST LIKE A WOMAN

Nobody feels any pain
Tonight as I stand inside the rain
Ev'rybody knows
That Baby's got new clothes
But lately I see her ribbons and her bows
Have fallen from her curls
She takes just like a woman, yes, she does
She makes love just like a woman, yes, she does
And she aches just like a woman
But she breaks just like a little girl

Queen Mary, she's my friend
Yes, I believe I'll go see her again
Nobody has to guess
That Baby can't be blessed
Till she sees finally that she's like all the rest
With her fog, her amphetamine and her pearls
She takes just like a woman, yes, she does
She makes love just like a woman, yes, she does
And she aches just like a woman
But she breaks just like a little girl

It was raining from the first
And I was dying there of thirst
So I came in here
And your long-time curse hurts
But what's worse
Is this pain in here
I can't stay in here
Ain't it clear that——

I just can't fit
Yes, I believe it's time for us to quit
When we meet again
Introduced as friends
Please don't let on that you knew me when
I was hungry and it was your world
Ah, you fake just like a woman, yes, you do
You make love just like a woman, yes, you do
Then you ache just like a woman
But you break just like a little girl

I'LL KEEP IT WITH MINE

You will search, babe
At any cost
But how long, babe
Can you search for what's not lost?
Everybody will help you
Some people are very kind
But if I can save you any time
Come on, give it to me
I'll keep it with mine

I can't help it
If you might think I'm odd
If I say I'm not loving you for what you are
But for what you're not
Everybody will help you
Discover what you set out to find
But if I can save you any time
Come on, give it to me
I'll keep it with mine

The train leaves
At half past ten
But it'll be back tomorrow
Same time again
The conductor he's weary
He's still stuck on the line
But if I can save you any time
Come on, give it to me
I'll keep it with mine

ALL ALONG THE WATCHTOWER

"There must be some way out of here," said the joker to the thief
"There's too much confusion, I can't get no relief
Businessmen, they drink my wine, plowmen dig my earth
None of them along the line know what any of it is worth"

"No reason to get excited," the thief, he kindly spoke
"There are many here among us who feel that life is but a joke
But you and I, we've been through that, and this is not our fate
So let us not talk falsely now, the hour is getting late"

All along the watchtower, princes kept the view
While all the women came and went, barefoot servants, too

Outside in the distance a wildcat did growl
Two riders were approaching, the wind began to howl

I PITY THE POOR IMMIGRANT

I pity the poor immigrant
Who wishes he would've stayed home
Who uses all his power to do evil
But in the end is always left so alone
That man whom with his fingers cheats
And who lies with ev'ry breath
Who passionately hates his life
And likewise, fears his death

I pity the poor immigrant
Whose strength is spent in vain
Whose heaven is like Ironsides
Whose tears are like rain
Who eats but is not satisfied
Who hears but does not see
Who falls in love with wealth itself
And turns his back on me

I pity the poor immigrant
Who tramples through the mud
Who fills his mouth with laughing
And who builds his town with blood
Whose visions in the final end
Must shatter like the glass
I pity the poor immigrant
When his gladness comes to pass

THE WICKED MESSENGER

There was a wicked messenger
From Eli he did come
With a mind that multiplied the smallest matter
When questioned who had sent for him
He answered with his thumb
For his tongue it could not speak, but only flatter

He stayed behind the assembly hall
It was there he made his bed
Oftentimes he could be seen returning
Until one day he just appeared
With a note in his hand which read
"The soles of my feet, I swear they're burning"

Oh, the leaves began to fallin'
And the seas began to part
And the people that confronted him were many
And he was told but these few words
Which opened up his heart
"If ye cannot bring good news, then don't bring any"

LAY, LADY, LAY

Lay, lady, lay, lay across my big brass bed
Lay, lady, lay, lay across my big brass bed
Whatever colors you have in your mind
I'll show them to you and you'll see them shine

Lay, lady, lay, lay across my big brass bed
Stay, lady, stay, stay with your man awhile
Until the break of day, let me see you make him smile
His clothes are dirty but his hands are clean
And you're the best thing that he's ever seen

Stay, lady, stay, stay with your man awhile
Why wait any longer for the world to begin
You can have your cake and eat it too
Why wait any longer for the one you love
When he's standing in front of you

Lay, lady, lay, lay across my big brass bed
Stay, lady, stay, stay while the night is still ahead
I long to see you in the morning light
I long to reach for you in the night
Stay, lady, stay, stay while the night is still ahead

IF NOT FOR YOU

If not for you
Babe, I couldn't find the door
Couldn't even see the floor
I'd be sad and blue
If not for you

If not for you
Babe, I'd lay awake all night
Wait for the mornin' light
To shine in through
But it would not be new
If not for you

If not for you
My sky would fall
Rain would gather too
Without your love I'd be nowhere at all
I'd be lost if not for you
And you know it's true

If not for you
My sky would fall
Rain would gather too
Without your love I'd be nowhere at all
Oh! what would I do
If not for you

If not for you
Winter would have no spring
Couldn't hear the robin sing
I just wouldn't have a clue
Anyway it wouldn't ring true
If not for you

TIME PASSES SLOWLY

Time passes slowly up here in the mountains
We sit beside bridges and walk beside fountains
Catch the wild fishes that float through the stream
Time passes slowly when you're lost in a dream

Once I had a sweetheart, she was fine and good-lookin'
We sat in her kitchen while her mama was cookin'
Stared out the window to the stars high above
Time passes slowly when you're searchin' for love

Ain't no reason to go in a wagon to town
Ain't no reason to go to the fair
Ain't no reason to go up, ain't no reason to go down
Ain't no reason to go anywhere

Time passes slowly up here in the daylight
We stare straight ahead and try so hard to stay right
Like the red rose of summer that blooms in the day
Time passes slowly and fades away

WENT TO SEE THE GYPSY

Went to see the gypsy
Stayin' in a big hotel
He smiled when he saw me coming
And he said, "Well, well, well"
His room was dark and crowded
Lights were low and dim
"How are you?" he said to me
I said it back to him

I went down to the lobby
To make a small call out
A pretty dancing girl was there
And she began to shout
"Go on back to see the gypsy
He can move you from the rear
Drive you from your fear
Bring you through the mirror
He did it in Las Vegas
And he can do it here"

Outside the lights were shining
On the river of tears
I watched them from the distance
With music in my ears

I went back to see the gypsy
It was nearly early dawn
The gypsy's door was open wide
But the gypsy was gone
And that pretty dancing girl
She could not be found
So I watched that sun come rising
From that little Minnesota town

THE MAN IN ME

The man in me will do nearly any task
And as for compensation, there's little he would ask
Take a woman like you
To get through to the man in me

Storm clouds are raging all around my door
I think to myself I might not take it anymore
Take a woman like your kind
To find the man in me

But, oh, what a wonderful feeling
Just to know that you are near
Sets my heart a-reeling
From my toes up to my ears

The man in me will hide sometimes to keep from bein' seen
But that's just because he doesn't want to turn into some machine
Took a woman like you
To get through to the man in me

WATCHING THE RIVER FLOW

What's the matter with me
I don't have much to say
Daylight sneakin' through the window
And I'm still in this all-night café
Walkin' to and fro beneath the moon
Out to where the trucks are rollin' slow
To sit down on this bank of sand
And watch the river flow

Wish I was back in the city
Instead of this old bank of sand
With the sun beating down over the chimney tops
And the one I love so close at hand
If I had wings and I could fly
I know where I would go
But right now I'll just sit here so contentedly
And watch the river flow

People disagreeing on all just about everything, yeah
Makes you stop and all wonder why
Why only yesterday I saw somebody on the street
Who just couldn't help but cry
Oh, this ol' river keeps on rollin', though
No matter what gets in the way and which way the wind does blow
And as long as it does I'll just sit here
And watch the river flow

People disagreeing everywhere you look
Makes you wanna stop and read a book
Why only yesterday I saw somebody on the street
That was really shook
But this ol' river keeps on rollin', though
No matter what gets in the way and which way the wind does blow
And as long as it does I'll just sit here
And watch the river flow

Watch the river flow
Watchin' the river flow
Watchin' the river flow
But I'll sit down on this bank of sand
And watch the river flow

WHEN I PAINT MY MASTERPIECE

Oh, the streets of Rome are filled with rubble
Ancient footprints are everywhere
You can almost think that you're seein' double
On a cold, dark night on the Spanish Stairs
Got to hurry on back to my hotel room
Where I've got me a date with Botticelli's niece
She promised that she'd be right there with me
When I paint my masterpiece

Oh, the hours I've spent inside the Coliseum
Dodging lions and wastin' time
Oh, those mighty kings of the jungle, I could hardly stand to see 'em
Yes, it sure has been a long, hard climb
Train wheels runnin' through the back of my memory
When I ran on the hilltop following a pack of wild geese
Someday, everything is gonna be smooth like a rhapsody
When I paint my masterpiece

Sailin' round the world in a dirty gondola
Oh, to be back in the land of Coca-Cola!

I left Rome and landed in Brussels
On a plane ride so bumpy that I almost cried
Clergymen in uniform and young girls pullin' muscles
Everyone was there to greet me when I stepped inside
Newspapermen eating candy
Had to be held down by big police
Someday, everything is gonna be diff'rent
When I paint my masterpiece

TEARS OF RAGE

(with Richard Manuel)

We carried you in our arms
On Independence Day
And now you'd throw us all aside
And put us on our way
Oh what dear daughter 'neath the sun
Would treat a father so
To wait upon him hand and foot
And always tell him, "No"?
Tears of rage, tears of grief
Why must I always be the thief?
Come to me now, you know
We're so alone
And life is brief

We pointed out the way to go
And scratched your name in sand
Though you just thought it was nothing more
Than a place for you to stand
Now, I want you to know that while we watched
You discover there was no one true
Most ev'rybody really thought
It was a childish thing to do
Tears of rage, tears of grief
Must I always be the thief?
Come to me now, you know
We're so low
And life is brief

It was all very painless
When you went out to receive
All that false instruction
Which we never could believe
And now the heart is filled with gold
As if it was a purse
But, oh, what kind of love is this
Which goes from bad to worse?
Tears of rage, tears of grief
Must I always be the thief?
Come to me now, you know
We're so low
And life is brief

TOO MUCH OF NOTHING

Now, too much of nothing
Can make a man feel ill at ease
One man's temper might rise
While another man's temper might freeze
In the day of confession
We cannot mock a soul
Oh, when there's too much of nothing
No one has control

Say hello to Valerie
Say hello to Vivian
Send them all my salary
On the waters of oblivion

Too much of nothing
Can make a man abuse a king
He can walk the streets and boast like most
But he wouldn't know a thing
Now, it's all been done before
It's all been written in the book
But when there's too much of nothing
Nobody should look

Say hello to Valerie
Say hello to Vivian
Send them all my salary
On the waters of oblivion

Too much of nothing
Can turn a man into a liar
It can cause one man to sleep on nails
And another man to eat fire
Ev'rybody's doin' somethin'
I heard it in a dream
But when there's too much of nothing
It just makes a fella mean

Say hello to Valerie
Say hello to Vivian
Send them all my salary
On the waters of oblivion

YOU AIN'T GOIN' NOWHERE

Clouds so swift
Rain won't lift
Gate won't close
Railings froze
Get your mind off wintertime
You ain't goin' nowhere
Whoo-ee! Ride me high
Tomorrow's the day
My bride's gonna come
Oh, oh, are we gonna fly
Down in the easy chair!

I don't care
How many letters they sent
Morning came and morning went
Pick up your money
And pack up your tent
You ain't goin' nowhere
Whoo-ee! Ride me high
Tomorrow's the day
My bride's gonna come
Oh, oh, are we gonna fly
Down in the easy chair!

Buy me a flute
And a gun that shoots
Tailgates and substitutes
Strap yourself
To the tree with roots
You ain't goin' nowhere
Whoo-ee! Ride me high
Tomorrow's the day
My bride's gonna come
Oh, oh, are we gonna fly
Down in the easy chair!

Genghis Khan
He could not keep
All his kings
Supplied with sleep
We'll climb that hill no matter how steep
When we get up to it
Whoo-ee! Ride me high
Tomorrow's the day
My bride's gonna come
Oh, oh, are we gonna fly
Down in the easy chair!

THIS WHEEL'S ON FIRE

(with Rick Danko)

If your mem'ry serves you well
We were goin' to meet again and wait
So I'm goin' to unpack all my things
And sit before it gets too late
No man alive will come to you
With another tale to tell
But you know that we shall meet again
If your mem'ry serves you well
This wheel's on fire
Rolling down the road
Best notify my next of kin
This wheel shall explode!

If your mem'ry serves you well
I was goin' to confiscate your lace
And wrap it up in a sailor's knot
And hide it in your case
If I knew for sure that it was yours . . .
But it was oh so hard to tell
But you knew that we would meet again
If your mem'ry serves you well
This wheel's on fire
Rolling down the road
Best notify my next of kin
This wheel shall explode!

If your mem'ry serves you well
You'll remember you're the one
That called on me to call on them
To get you your favors done
And after ev'ry plan had failed
And there was nothing more to tell
You knew that we would meet again
If your mem'ry served you well
This wheel's on fire
Rolling down the road
Best notify my next of kin
This wheel shall explode!

QUINN THE ESKIMO (THE MIGHTY QUINN)

Ev'rybody's building the big ships and the boats
Some are building monuments
Others, jotting down notes
Ev'rybody's in despair
Ev'ry girl and boy
But when Quinn the Eskimo gets here
Ev'rybody's gonna jump for joy
Come all without, come all within
You'll not see nothing like the mighty Quinn

I like to do just like the rest, I like my sugar sweet
But guarding fumes and making haste
It ain't my cup of meat
Ev'rybody's 'neath the trees
Feeding pigeons on a limb
But when Quinn the Eskimo gets here
All the pigeons gonna run to him
Come all without, come all within
You'll not see nothing like the mighty Quinn

A cat's meow and a cow's moo, I can recite 'em all
Just tell me where it hurts yuh, honey
And I'll tell you who to call
Nobody can get no sleep
There's someone on ev'ryone's toes
But when Quinn the Eskimo gets here
Ev'rybody's gonna wanna doze
Come all without, come all within
You'll not see nothing like the mighty Quinn

I SHALL BE RELEASED

They say ev'rything can be replaced
Yet ev'ry distance is not near
So I remember ev'ry face
Of ev'ry man who put me here
I see my light come shining
From the west unto the east
Any day now, any day now
I shall be released

They say ev'ry man needs protection
They say ev'ry man must fall
Yet I swear I see my reflection
Some place so high above this wall
I see my light come shining
From the west unto the east
Any day now, any day now
I shall be released

Standing next to me in this lonely crowd
Is a man who swears he's not to blame
All day long I hear him shout so loud
Crying out that he was framed
I see my light come shining
From the west unto the east
Any day now, any day now
I shall be released

BILLY

There's guns across the river aimin' at ya
Lawman on your trail, he'd like to catch ya
Bounty hunters, too, they'd like to get ya
Billy, they don't like you to be so free

Campin' out all night on the berenda
Dealin' cards 'til dawn in the hacienda
Up to Boot Hill they'd like to send ya
Billy, don't you turn your back on me

Playin' around with some sweet señorita
Into her dark hallway she will lead ya
In some lonesome shadows she will greet ya
Billy, you're so far away from home

There's eyes behind the mirrors in empty places
Bullet holes and scars between the spaces
There's always one more notch and ten more paces
Billy, and you're walkin' all alone

They say that Pat Garrett's got your number
So sleep with one eye open when you slumber
Every little sound just might be thunder
Thunder from the barrel of his gun

Guitars will play your grand finale
Down in some Tularosa alley
Maybe in the Rio Pecos valley
Billy, you're so far away from home

There's always some new stranger sneakin' glances
Some trigger-happy fool willin' to take chances
And some old whore from San Pedro to make advances
Advances on your spirit and your soul

The businessmen from Taos want you to go down
They've hired Pat Garrett to force a showdown
Billy, don't it make ya feel so low-down
To be shot down by the man who was your friend?

Hang on to your woman if you got one
Remember in El Paso, once, you shot one
She may have been a whore, but she was a hot one
Billy, you been runnin' for so long

Guitars will play your grand finale
Down in some Tularosa alley
Maybe in the Rio Pecos valley
Billy, you're so far away from home

KNOCKIN' ON HEAVEN'S DOOR

Mama, take this badge off of me
I can't use it anymore
It's gettin' dark, too dark for me to see
I feel like I'm knockin' on heaven's door

Knock, knock, knockin' on heaven's door
Knock, knock, knockin' on heaven's door
Knock, knock, knockin' on heaven's door
Knock, knock, knockin' on heaven's door

Mama, put my guns in the ground
I can't shoot them anymore
That long black cloud is comin' down
I feel like I'm knockin' on heaven's door

Knock, knock, knockin' on heaven's door
Knock, knock, knockin' on heaven's door
Knock, knock, knockin' on heaven's door
Knock, knock, knockin' on heaven's door

FOREVER YOUNG

May God bless and keep you always
May your wishes all come true
May you always do for others
And let others do for you
May you build a ladder to the stars
And climb on every rung
May you stay forever young
Forever young, forever young
May you stay forever young

May you grow up to be righteous
May you grow up to be true
May you always know the truth
And see the lights surrounding you
May you always be courageous
Stand upright and be strong
May you stay forever young
Forever young, forever young
May you stay forever young

May your hands always be busy
May your feet always be swift
May you have a strong foundation
When the winds of changes shift
May your heart always be joyful
May your song always be sung
May you stay forever young
Forever young, forever young
May you stay forever young

TANGLED UP IN BLUE

Early one mornin' the sun was shinin'
I was layin' in bed
Wond'rin' if she'd changed at all
If her hair was still red
Her folks they said our lives together
Sure was gonna be rough
They never did like Mama's homemade dress
Papa's bankbook wasn't big enough
And I was standin' on the side of the road
Rain fallin' on my shoes
Heading out for the East Coast
Lord knows I've paid some dues gettin' through
Tangled up in blue

She was married when we first met
Soon to be divorced
I helped her out of a jam, I guess
But I used a little too much force
We drove that car as far as we could
Abandoned it out West
Split up on a dark sad night
Both agreeing it was best
She turned around to look at me
As I was walkin' away
I heard her say over my shoulder
"We'll meet again someday on the avenue"
Tangled up in blue

I had a job in the great north woods
Working as a cook for a spell
But I never did like it all that much
And one day the ax just fell
So I drifted down to New Orleans
Where I happened to be employed
Workin' for a while on a fishin' boat
Right outside of Delacroix
But all the while I was alone
The past was close behind
I seen a lot of women
But she never escaped my mind, and I just grew
Tangled up in blue

She was workin' in a topless place
And I stopped in for a beer
I just kept lookin' at the side of her face
In the spotlight so clear
And later on as the crowd thinned out
I's just about to do the same
She was standing there in back of my chair
Said to me, "Don't I know your name?"
I muttered somethin' underneath my breath
She studied the lines on my face
I must admit I felt a little uneasy
When she bent down to tie the laces of my shoe
Tangled up in blue

She lit a burner on the stove
And offered me a pipe
"I thought you'd never say hello," she said
"You look like the silent type"
Then she opened up a book of poems
And handed it to me
Written by an Italian poet
From the thirteenth century
And every one of them words rang true
And glowed like burnin' coal
Pourin' off of every page
Like it was written in my soul from me to you
Tangled up in blue

I lived with them on Montague Street
In a basement down the stairs
There was music in the cafés at night
And revolution in the air
Then he started into dealing with slaves
And something inside of him died
She had to sell everything she owned
And froze up inside
And when finally the bottom fell out
I became withdrawn
The only thing I knew how to do
Was to keep on keepin' on like a bird that flew
Tangled up in blue

So now I'm goin' back again
I got to get to her somehow
All the people we used to know
They're an illusion to me now
Some are mathematicians
Some are carpenters' wives
Don't know how it all got started
I don't know what they're doin' with their lives
But me, I'm still on the road
Headin' for another joint
We always did feel the same
We just saw it from a different point of view
Tangled up in blue

SIMPLE TWIST OF FATE

They sat together in the park
As the evening sky grew dark
She looked at him and he felt a spark tingle to his bones
'Twas then he felt alone and wished that he'd gone straight
And watched out for a simple twist of fate

They walked along by the old canal
A little confused, I remember well
And stopped into a strange hotel with a neon burnin' bright
He felt the heat of the night hit him like a freight train
Moving with a simple twist of fate

A saxophone someplace far off played
As she was walkin' by the arcade
As the light bust through a beat-up shade where he was wakin' up
She dropped a coin into the cup of a blind man at the gate
And forgot about a simple twist of fate

He woke up, the room was bare
He didn't see her anywhere
He told himself he didn't care, pushed the window open wide
Felt an emptiness inside to which he just could not relate
Brought on by a simple twist of fate

He hears the ticking of the clocks
And walks along with a parrot that talks
Hunts her down by the waterfront docks where the sailors all come in
Maybe she'll pick him out again, how long must he wait
Once more for a simple twist of fate

People tell me it's a sin
To know and feel too much within
I still believe she was my twin, but I lost the ring
She was born in spring, but I was born too late
Blame it on a simple twist of fate

IDIOT WIND

Someone's got it in for me, they're planting stories in the press
Whoever it is I wish they'd cut it out but when they will I can only guess
They say I shot a man named Gray and took his wife to Italy
She inherited a million bucks and when she died it came to me
I can't help it if I'm lucky

People see me all the time and they just can't remember how to act
Their minds are filled with big ideas, images and distorted facts
Even you, yesterday you had to ask me where it was at
I couldn't believe after all these years, you didn't know me better than that
Sweet lady

Idiot wind, blowing every time you move your mouth
Blowing down the backroads headin' south
Idiot wind, blowing every time you move your teeth
You're an idiot, babe
It's a wonder that you still know how to breathe

I ran into the fortune-teller, who said beware of lightning that might strike
I haven't known peace and quiet for so long I can't remember what it's like
There's a lone soldier on the cross, smoke pourin' out of a boxcar door
You didn't know it, you didn't think it could be done, in the final end he won the wars
After losin' every battle

I woke up on the roadside, daydreamin' 'bout the way things sometimes are
Visions of your chestnut mare shoot through my head and are makin' me see stars
You hurt the ones that I love best and cover up the truth with lies
One day you'll be in the ditch, flies buzzin' around your eyes
Blood on your saddle

Idiot wind, blowing through the flowers on your tomb
Blowing through the curtains in your room
Idiot wind, blowing every time you move your teeth
You're an idiot, babe
It's a wonder that you still know how to breathe

It was gravity which pulled us down and destiny which broke us apart
You tamed the lion in my cage but it just wasn't enough to change my heart
Now everything's a little upside down, as a matter of fact the wheels have stopped
What's good is bad, what's bad is good, you'll find out when you reach the top
You're on the bottom

I noticed at the ceremony, your corrupt ways had finally made you blind
I can't remember your face anymore, your mouth has changed, your eyes
    don't look into mine
The priest wore black on the seventh day and sat stone-faced while the building burned
I waited for you on the running boards, near the cypress trees, while the
    springtime turned
Slowly into autumn

Idiot wind, blowing like a circle around my skull
From the Grand Coulee Dam to the Capitol
Idiot wind, blowing every time you move your teeth
You're an idiot, babe
It's a wonder that you still know how to breathe

I can't feel you anymore, I can't even touch the books you've read
Every time I crawl past your door, I been wishin' I was somebody else instead
Down the highway, down the tracks, down the road to ecstasy
I followed you beneath the stars, hounded by your memory
And all your ragin' glory

I been double-crossed now for the very last time and now I'm finally free
I kissed goodbye the howling beast on the borderline which separated you from me
You'll never know the hurt I suffered nor the pain I rise above
And I'll never know the same about you, your holiness or your kind of love
And it makes me feel so sorry

Idiot wind, blowing through the buttons of our coats
Blowing through the letters that we wrote
Idiot wind, blowing through the dust upon our shelves
We're idiots, babe
It's a wonder we can even feed ourselves

SHELTER FROM THE STORM

'Twas in another lifetime, one of toil and blood
When blackness was a virtue and the road was full of mud
I came in from the wilderness, a creature void of form
"Come in," she said, "I'll give you shelter from the storm"

And if I pass this way again, you can rest assured
I'll always do my best for her, on that I give my word
In a world of steel-eyed death, and men who are fighting to be warm
"Come in," she said, "I'll give you shelter from the storm"

Not a word was spoke between us, there was little risk involved
Everything up to that point had been left unresolved
Try imagining a place where it's always safe and warm
"Come in," she said, "I'll give you shelter from the storm"

I was burned out from exhaustion, buried in the hail
Poisoned in the bushes an' blown out on the trail
Hunted like a crocodile, ravaged in the corn
"Come in," she said, "I'll give you shelter from the storm"

Suddenly I turned around and she was standin' there
With silver bracelets on her wrists and flowers in her hair
She walked up to me so gracefully and took my crown of thorns
"Come in," she said, "I'll give you shelter from the storm"

Now there's a wall between us, somethin' there's been lost
I took too much for granted, got my signals crossed
Just to think that it all began on a long-forgotten morn
"Come in," she said, "I'll give you shelter from the storm"

Well, the deputy walks on hard nails and the preacher rides a mount
But nothing really matters much, it's doom alone that counts
And the one-eyed undertaker, he blows a futile horn
"Come in," she said, "I'll give you shelter from the storm"

I've heard newborn babies wailin' like a mournin' dove
And old men with broken teeth stranded without love
Do I understand your question, man, is it hopeless and forlorn?
"Come in," she said, "I'll give you shelter from the storm"

In a little hilltop village, they gambled for my clothes
I bargained for salvation an' they gave me a lethal dose
I offered up my innocence and got repaid with scorn
"Come in," she said, "I'll give you shelter from the storm"

Well, I'm livin' in a foreign country but I'm bound to cross the line
Beauty walks a razor's edge, someday I'll make it mine
If I could only turn back the clock to when God and her were born
"Come in," she said, "I'll give you shelter from the storm"

HURRICANE

(with Jacques Levy)

Pistol shots ring out in the barroom night
Enter Patty Valentine from the upper hall
She sees the bartender in a pool of blood
Cries out, "My God, they killed them all!"
Here comes the story of the Hurricane
The man the authorities came to blame
For somethin' that he never done
Put in a prison cell, but one time he could-a been
The champion of the world

Three bodies lyin' there does Patty see
And another man named Bello, movin' around mysteriously
"I didn't do it," he says, and he throws up his hands
"I was only robbin' the register, I hope you understand
I saw them leavin'," he says, and he stops
"One of us had better call up the cops"
And so Patty calls the cops
And they arrive on the scene with their red lights flashin'
In the hot New Jersey night

Meanwhile, far away in another part of town
Rubin Carter and a couple of friends are drivin' around
Number one contender for the middleweight crown
Had no idea what kinda shit was about to go down
When a cop pulled him over to the side of the road
Just like the time before and the time before that
In Paterson that's just the way things go
If you're black you might as well not show up on the street
'Less you wanna draw the heat

Alfred Bello had a partner and he had a rap for the cops
Him and Arthur Dexter Bradley were just out prowlin' around
He said, "I saw two men runnin' out, they looked like middleweights
They jumped into a white car with out-of-state plates"
And Miss Patty Valentine just nodded her head
Cop said, "Wait a minute, boys, this one's not dead"
So they took him to the infirmary
And though this man could hardly see
They told him that he could identify the guilty men

Four in the mornin' and they haul Rubin in
Take him to the hospital and they bring him upstairs
The wounded man looks up through his one dyin' eye
Says, "Wha'd you bring him in here for? He ain't the guy!"
Yes, here's the story of the Hurricane
The man the authorities came to blame
For somethin' that he never done
Put in a prison cell, but one time he could-a been
The champion of the world

Four months later, the ghettos are in flame
Rubin's in South America, fightin' for his name
While Arthur Dexter Bradley's still in the robbery game
And the cops are puttin' the screws to him, lookin' for somebody to blame
"Remember that murder that happened in a bar?"
"Remember you said you saw the getaway car?"
"You think you'd like to play ball with the law?"
"Think it might-a been that fighter that you saw runnin' that night?"
"Don't forget that you are white"

Arthur Dexter Bradley said, "I'm really not sure"
Cops said, "A poor boy like you could use a break
We got you for the motel job and we're talkin' to your friend Bello
Now you don't wanta have to go back to jail, be a nice fellow
You'll be doin' society a favor
That sonofabitch is brave and gettin' braver
We want to put his ass in stir
We want to pin this triple murder on him
He ain't no Gentleman Jim"

Rubin could take a man out with just one punch
But he never did like to talk about it all that much
It's my work, he'd say, and I do it for pay
And when it's over I'd just as soon go on my way
Up to some paradise
Where the trout streams flow and the air is nice
And ride a horse along a trail
But then they took him to the jailhouse
Where they try to turn a man into a mouse

All of Rubin's cards were marked in advance
The trial was a pig-circus, he never had a chance
The judge made Rubin's witnesses drunkards from the slums
To the white folks who watched he was a revolutionary bum
And to the black folks he was just a crazy nigger
No one doubted that he pulled the trigger
And though they could not produce the gun
The D.A. said he was the one who did the deed
And the all-white jury agreed

Rubin Carter was falsely tried
The crime was murder "one," guess who testified?
Bello and Bradley and they both baldly lied
And the newspapers, they all went along for the ride
How can the life of such a man
Be in the palm of some fool's hand?
To see him obviously framed
Couldn't help but make me feel ashamed to live in a land
Where justice is a game

Now all the criminals in their coats and their ties
Are free to drink martinis and watch the sun rise
While Rubin sits like Buddha in a ten-foot cell
An innocent man in a living hell
That's the story of the Hurricane
But it won't be over till they clear his name
And give him back the time he's done
Put in a prison cell, but one time he could-a been
The champion of the world

ROMANCE IN DURANGO

(with Jacques Levy)

Hot chili peppers in the blistering sun
Dust on my face and my cape
Me and Magdalena on the run
I think this time we shall escape

Sold my guitar to the baker's son
For a few crumbs and a place to hide
But I can get another one
And I'll play for Magdalena as we ride

No llores, mi querida
Dios nos vigila
Soon the horse will take us to Durango
Agarrame, mi vida
Soon the desert will be gone
Soon you will be dancing the fandango

Past the Aztec ruins and the ghosts of our people
Hoofbeats like castanets on stone
At night I dream of bells in the village steeple
Then I see the bloody face of Ramon

Was it me that shot him down in the cantina
Was it my hand that held the gun?
Come, let us fly, my Magdalena
The dogs are barking and what's done is done

No llores, mi querida
Dios nos vigila
Soon the horse will take us to Durango
Agarrame, mi vida
Soon the desert will be gone
Soon you will be dancing the fandango

At the corrida we'll sit in the shade
And watch the young torero stand alone
We'll drink tequila where our grandfathers stayed
When they rode with Villa into Torreón

Then the padre will recite the prayers of old
In the little church this side of town
I will wear new boots and an earring of gold
You'll shine with diamonds in your wedding gown

The way is long but the end is near
Already the fiesta has begun
The face of God will appear
With His serpent eyes of obsidian

No llores, mi querida
Dio nos vigila
Soon the horse will take us to Durango
Agarrame, mi vida
Soon the desert will be gone
Soon you will be dancing the fandango

Was that the thunder that I heard?
My head is vibrating, I feel a sharp pain
Come sit by me, don't say a word
Oh, can it be that I am slain?

Quick, Magdalena, take my gun
Look up in the hills, that flash of light
Aim well my little one
We may not make it through the night

No llores, mi querida
Dios nos vigila
Soon the horse will take us to Durango
Agarrame, mi vida
Soon the desert will be gone
Soon you will be dancing the fandango

CHANGING OF THE GUARDS

Sixteen years
Sixteen banners united over the field
Where the good shepherd grieves
Desperate men, desperate women divided
Spreading their wings 'neath the falling leaves

Fortune calls
I stepped forth from the shadows, to the marketplace
Merchants and thieves, hungry for power, my last deal gone down
She's smelling sweet like the meadows where she was born
On midsummer's eve, near the tower

The cold-blooded moon
The captain waits above the celebration
Sending his thoughts to a beloved maid
Whose ebony face is beyond communication
The captain is down but still believing that his love will be repaid

They shaved her head
She was torn between Jupiter and Apollo
A messenger arrived with a black nightingale
I seen her on the stairs and I couldn't help but follow
Follow her down past the fountain where they lifted her veil

I stumbled to my feet
I rode past destruction in the ditches
With the stitches still mending 'neath a heart-shaped tattoo
Renegade priests and treacherous young witches
Were handing out the flowers that I'd given to you

The palace of mirrors
Where dog soldiers are reflected
The endless road and the wailing of chimes
The empty rooms where her memory is protected
Where the angels' voices whisper to the souls of previous times

She wakes him up
Forty-eight hours later, the sun is breaking
Near broken chains, mountain laurel and rolling rocks
She's begging to know what measures he now will be taking
He's pulling her down and she's clutching on to his long golden locks

Gentlemen, he said
I don't need your organization, I've shined your shoes
I've moved your mountains and marked your cards
But Eden is burning, either brace yourself for elimination
Or else your hearts must have the courage for the changing of the guards

Peace will come
With tranquillity and splendor on the wheels of fire
But will bring us no reward when her false idols fall
And cruel death surrenders with its pale ghost retreating
Between the King and the Queen of Swords

SEÑOR
(TALES OF YANKEE POWER)

Señor, señor, do you know where we're headin'?
Lincoln County Road or Armageddon?
Seems like I been down this way before
Is there any truth in that, señor?

Señor, señor, do you know where she is hidin'?
How long are we gonna be ridin'?
How long must I keep my eyes glued to the door?
Will there be any comfort there, señor?

There's a wicked wind still blowin' on that upper deck
There's an iron cross still hanging down from around her neck
There's a marchin' band still playin' in that vacant lot
Where she held me in her arms one time and said, "Forget me not"

Señor, señor, I can see that painted wagon
I can smell the tail of the dragon
Can't stand the suspense anymore
Can you tell me who to contact here, señor?

Well, the last thing I remember before I stripped and kneeled
Was that trainload of fools bogged down in a magnetic field
A gypsy with a broken flag and a flashing ring
Said, "Son, this ain't a dream no more, it's the real thing"

Señor, señor, you know their hearts is as hard as leather
Well, give me a minute, let me get it together
I just gotta pick myself up off the floor
I'm ready when you are, señor

Señor, señor, let's disconnect these cables
Overturn these tables
This place don't make sense to me no more
Can you tell me what we're waiting for, señor?

GOTTA SERVE SOMEBODY

You may be an ambassador to England or France
You may like to gamble, you might like to dance
You may be the heavyweight champion of the world
You may be a socialite with a long string of pearls

But you're gonna have to serve somebody, yes indeed
You're gonna have to serve somebody
Well, it may be the devil or it may be the Lord
But you're gonna have to serve somebody

You might be a rock 'n' roll addict prancing on the stage
You might have drugs at your command, women in a cage
You may be a businessman or some high-degree thief
They may call you Doctor or they may call you Chief

But you're gonna have to serve somebody, yes indeed
You're gonna have to serve somebody
Well, it may be the devil or it may be the Lord
But you're gonna have to serve somebody

You may be a state trooper, you might be a young Turk
You may be the head of some big TV network
You may be rich or poor, you may be blind or lame
You may be living in another country under another name

But you're gonna have to serve somebody, yes indeed
You're gonna have to serve somebody
Well, it may be the devil or it may be the Lord
But you're gonna have to serve somebody

You may be a construction worker working on a home
You may be living in a mansion or you might live in a dome
You might own guns and you might even own tanks
You might be somebody's landlord, you might even own banks

But you're gonna have to serve somebody, yes indeed
You're gonna have to serve somebody
Well, it may be the devil or it may be the Lord
But you're gonna have to serve somebody

You may be a preacher with your spiritual pride
You may be a city councilman taking bribes on the side
You may be workin' in a barbershop, you may know how to cut hair
You may be somebody's mistress, may be somebody's heir

But you're gonna have to serve somebody, yes indeed
You're gonna have to serve somebody
Well, it may be the devil or it may be the Lord
But you're gonna have to serve somebody

Might like to wear cotton, might like to wear silk
Might like to drink whiskey, might like to drink milk
You might like to eat caviar, you might like to eat bread
You may be sleeping on the floor, sleeping in a king-sized bed

But you're gonna have to serve somebody, yes indeed
You're gonna have to serve somebody
Well, it may be the devil or it may be the Lord
But you're gonna have to serve somebody

You may call me Terry, you may call me Timmy
You may call me Bobby, you may call me Zimmy
You may call me R.J., you may call me Ray
You may call me anything but no matter what you say

You're gonna have to serve somebody, yes indeed
You're gonna have to serve somebody
Well, it may be the devil or it may be the Lord
But you're gonna have to serve somebody

SLOW TRAIN

Sometimes I feel so low-down and disgusted
Can't help but wonder what's happenin' to my companions
Are they lost or are they found
Have they counted the cost it'll take to bring down
All their earthly principles they're gonna have to abandon?
There's a slow, slow train comin' up around the bend

I had a woman down in Alabama
She was a backwoods girl, but she sure was realistic
She said, "Boy, without a doubt
Have to quit your mess and straighten out
You could die down here, be just another accident statistic"
There's a slow, slow train comin' up around the bend

All that foreign oil controlling American soil
Look around you, it's just bound to make you embarrassed
Sheiks walkin' around like kings
Wearing fancy jewels and nose rings
Deciding America's future from Amsterdam and to Paris
And there's a slow, slow train comin' up around the bend

Man's ego is inflated, his laws are outdated, they don't apply no more
You can't rely no more to be standin' around waitin'
In the home of the brave
Jefferson turnin' over in his grave
Fools glorifying themselves, trying to manipulate Satan
And there's a slow, slow train comin' up around the bend

Big-time negotiators, false healers and woman haters
Masters of the bluff and masters of the proposition
But the enemy I see
Wears a cloak of decency
All nonbelievers and men stealers talkin' in the name of religion
And there's a slow, slow train comin' up around the bend

People starving and thirsting, grain elevators are bursting
Oh, you know it costs more to store the food than it do to give it
They say lose your inhibitions
Follow your own ambitions
They talk about a life of brotherly love show me someone who knows how to live it
There's a slow, slow train comin' up around the bend

Well, my baby went to Illinois with some bad-talkin' boy she could destroy
A real suicide case, but there was nothin' I could do to stop it
I don't care about economy
I don't care about astronomy
But it sure do bother me to see my loved ones turning into puppets
There's a slow, slow train comin' up around the bend

WHAT CAN I DO FOR YOU?

You have given everything to me
What can I do for You?
You have given me eyes to see
What can I do for You?

Pulled me out of bondage and You made me renewed inside
Filled up a hunger that had always been denied
Opened up a door no man can shut and You opened it up so wide
And You've chosen me to be among the few
What can I do for You?

You have laid down Your life for me
What can I do for You?
You have explained every mystery
What can I do for You?

Soon as a man is born, you know the sparks begin to fly
He gets wise in his own eyes and he's made to believe a lie
Who would deliver him from the death he's bound to die?
Well, You've done it all and there's no more anyone can pretend to do
What can I do for You?

You have given all there is to give
What can I do for You?
You have given me life to live
How can I live for You?

I know all about poison, I know all about fiery darts
I don't care how rough the road is, show me where it starts
Whatever pleases You, tell it to my heart
Well, I don't deserve it but I sure did make it through
What can I do for You?

THE GROOM'S STILL WAITING AT THE ALTAR

Prayed in the ghetto with my face in the cement
Heard the last moan of a boxer, seen the massacre of the innocent
Felt around for the light switch, became nauseated
She was walking down the hallway while the walls deteriorated

West of the Jordan, east of the Rock of Gibraltar
I see the turning of the page
Curtain risin' on a new age
See the groom still waitin' at the altar

Try to be pure at heart, they arrest you for robbery
Mistake your shyness for aloofness, your silence for snobbery
Got the message this morning, the one that was sent to me
About the madness of becomin' what one was never meant to be

West of the Jordan, east of the Rock of Gibraltar
I see the burning of the stage
Curtain risin' on a new age
See the groom still waitin' at the altar

Don't know what I can say about Claudette that wouldn't come back to haunt me
Finally had to give her up 'bout the time she began to want me
But I know God has mercy on them who are slandered and humiliated
I'd a-done anything for that woman if she didn't make me feel so obligated

West of the Jordan, east of the Rock of Gibraltar
I see the burning of the cage
Curtain risin' on a new stage
See the groom still waitin' at the altar

Put your hand on my head, baby, do I have a temperature?
I see people who are supposed to know better standin' around like furniture
There's a wall between you and what you want and you got to leap it
Tonight you got the power to take it, tomorrow you won't have the power to keep it

West of the Jordan, east of the Rock of Gibraltar
I see the burning of the stage
Curtain risin' on a new age
See the groom still waitin' at the altar

Cities on fire, phones out of order
They're killing nuns and soldiers, there's fighting on the border
What can I say about Claudette? Ain't seen her since January
She could be respectfully married or running a whorehouse in Buenos Aires

West of the Jordan, east of the Rock of Gibraltar
I see the burning of the stage
Curtain risin' on a new age
See the groom still waitin' at the altar

EVERY GRAIN OF SAND

In the time of my confession, in the hour of my deepest need
When the pool of tears beneath my feet flood every newborn seed
There's a dyin' voice within me reaching out somewhere
Toiling in the danger and in the morals of despair

Don't have the inclination to look back on any mistake
Like Cain, I now behold this chain of events that I must break
In the fury of the moment I can see the Master's hand
In every leaf that trembles, in every grain of sand

Oh, the flowers of indulgence and the weeds of yesteryear
Like criminals, they have choked the breath of conscience and good cheer
The sun beat down upon the steps of time to light the way
To ease the pain of idleness and the memory of decay

I gaze into the doorway of temptation's angry flame
And every time I pass that way I always hear my name
Then onward in my journey I come to understand
That every hair is numbered like every grain of sand

I have gone from rags to riches in the sorrow of the night
In the violence of a summer's dream, in the chill of a wintry light
In the bitter dance of loneliness fading into space
In the broken mirror of innocence on each forgotten face

I hear the ancient footsteps like the motion of the sea
Sometimes I turn, there's someone there, other times it's only me
I am hanging in the balance of the reality of man
Like every sparrow falling, like every grain of sand

CARIBBEAN WIND

She was the rose of Sharon from paradise lost
From the city of seven hills near the place of the cross
I was playing a show in Miami in the theater of divine comedy
Told about Jesus, told about the rain
She told me about the jungle where her brothers were slain
By a man who danced on the roof of the embassy

Was she a child or a woman, I can't say which
From one to another she could easily switch
We went into the wall to where the long arm of the law could not reach
Could I been used and played as a pawn?
It certainly was possible as the gay night wore on
Where men bathed in perfume and celebrated free speech

And them Caribbean winds still blow from Nassau to Mexico
Fanning the flames in the furnace of desire
And them distant ships of liberty on them iron waves so bold and free
Bringing everything that's near to me nearer to the fire

She looked into my soul through the clothes that I wore
She said, "We got a mutual friend over by the door
And you know he's got our best interest in mind"
He was well connected but her heart was a snare
And she had left him to die in there
There were payments due and he was a little behind

The cry of the peacock, flies buzz my head
Ceiling fan broken, there's a heat in my bed
Street band playing "Nearer My God to Thee"
We met at the steeple where the mission bells ring
She said, "I know what you're thinking, but there ain't a thing
You can do about it, so let us just agree to agree"

And them Caribbean winds still blow from Nassau to Mexico
Fanning the flames in the furnace of desire
And them distant ships of liberty on them iron waves so bold and free
Bringing everything that's near to me nearer to the fire

Atlantic City by the cold grey sea
I hear a voice crying, "Daddy," I always think it's for me
But it's only the silence in the buttermilk hills that call
Every new messenger brings evil report
'Bout armies on the march and time that is short
And famines and earthquakes and hatred written upon walls

Would I have married her? I don't know, I suppose
She had bells in her braids and they hung to her toes
But I kept hearing my name and had to be movin' on
I saw screws break loose, saw the devil pound tin
I saw a house in the country being torn from within
I heard my ancestors calling from the land far beyond

And them Caribbean winds still blow from Nassau to Mexico
Fanning the flames in the furnace of desire
And them distant ships of liberty on them iron waves so bold and free
Bringing everything that's near to me nearer to the fire

JOKERMAN

Standing on the waters casting your bread
While the eyes of the idol with the iron head are glowing
Distant ships sailing into the mist
You were born with a snake in both of your fists while a hurricane was blowing
Freedom just around the corner for you
But with the truth so far off, what good will it do?

Jokerman dance to the nightingale tune
Bird fly high by the light of the moon
Oh, oh, oh, Jokerman

So swiftly the sun sets in the sky
You rise up and say goodbye to no one
Fools rush in where angels fear to tread
Both of their futures, so full of dread, you don't show one
Shedding off one more layer of skin
Keeping one step ahead of the persecutor within

Jokerman dance to the nightingale tune
Bird fly high by the light of the moon
Oh, oh, oh, Jokerman

You're a man of the mountains, you can walk on the clouds
Manipulator of crowds, you're a dream twister
You're going to Sodom and Gomorrah
But what do you care? Ain't nobody there would want to marry your sister
Friend to the martyr, a friend to the woman of shame
You look into the fiery furnace, see the rich man without any name

Jokerman dance to the nightingale tune
Bird fly high by the light of the moon
Oh, oh, oh, Jokerman

Well, the Book of Leviticus and Deuteronomy
The law of the jungle and the sea are your only teachers
In the smoke of the twilight on a milk-white steed
Michelangelo indeed could've carved out your features
Resting in the fields, far from the turbulent space
Half asleep near the stars with a small dog licking your face

Jokerman dance to the nightingale tune
Bird fly high by the light of the moon
Oh, oh, oh, Jokerman

Well, the rifleman's stalking the sick and the lame
Preacherman seeks the same, who'll get there first is uncertain
Nightsticks and water cannons, tear gas, padlocks
Molotov cocktails and rocks behind every curtain
False-hearted judges dying in the webs that they spin
Only a matter of time 'til night comes steppin' in

Jokerman dance to the nightingale tune
Bird fly high by the light of the moon
Oh, oh, oh, Jokerman

It's a shadowy world, skies are slippery grey
A woman just gave birth to a prince today and dressed him in scarlet
He'll put the priest in his pocket, put the blade to the heat
Take the motherless children off the street and place them at the feet of a harlot
Oh, Jokerman, you know what he wants
Oh, Jokerman, you don't show any response

Jokerman dance to the nightingale tune
Bird fly high by the light of the moon
Oh, oh, oh, Jokerman

LICENSE TO KILL

Man thinks 'cause he rules the earth he can do with it as he please
And if things don't change soon, he will
Oh, man has invented his doom
First step was touching the moon

Now, there's a woman on my block
She just sit there as the night grows still
She say who gonna take away his license to kill?

Now, they take him and they teach him and they groom him for life
And they set him on a path where he's bound to get ill
Then they bury him with stars
Sell his body like they do used cars

Now, there's a woman on my block
She just sit there facin' the hill
She say who gonna take away his license to kill?

Now, he's hell-bent for destruction, he's afraid and confused
And his brain has been mismanaged with great skill
All he believes are his eyes
And his eyes, they just tell him lies

But there's a woman on my block
Sitting there in a cold chill
She say who gonna take away his license to kill?

Ya may be a noisemaker, spirit maker
Heartbreaker, backbreaker
Leave no stone unturned
May be an actor in a plot
That might be all that you got
'Til your error you clearly learn

Now he worships at an altar of a stagnant pool
And when he sees his reflection, he's fulfilled
Oh, man is opposed to fair play
He wants it all and he wants it his way

Now, there's a woman on my block
She just sit there as the night grows still
She say who gonna take away his license to kill?

BLIND WILLIE McTELL

Seen the arrow on the doorpost
Saying, "This land is condemned
All the way from New Orleans
To new Jerusalem"
I traveled through East Texas
Where many martyrs fell
And I can tell you one thing
Nobody can sing the blues
Like Blind Willie McTell

Well, I heard that hoot owl singing
As they were taking down the tents
The stars above the barren trees
Were his only audience
Them charcoal gypsy maidens
Can strut their feathers well
And I can tell you one thing
Nobody can sing the blues
Like Blind Willie McTell

There's a woman by the river
With some fine young handsome man
He's dressed up like a squire
Bootlegged whiskey in his hand
Some of them died in the battle
Some of them survived as well
And I can tell you one thing
Nobody can sing the blues
Like Blind Willie McTell

Well, God is in His heaven
And we all want what's His
But power and greed and corruptible seed
Seem to be all that there is
I'm gazing out the window
Of the St. James Hotel
And I can tell you one thing
Nobody can sing the blues
Like Blind Willie McTell

TIGHT CONNECTION TO MY HEART (HAS ANYBODY SEEN MY LOVE)

Well, I had to move fast
And I couldn't with you around my neck
I said I'd send for you and I did
What did you expect?
My hands are sweating
And we haven't even started yet
I'll go along with the charade
Until I can think my way out
I know it was all a big joke
Whatever it was about
Someday maybe
I'll remember to forget

I'm gonna get my coat
I feel the breath of a storm
There's something I've got to do tonight
You go inside and stay warm

Has anybody seen my love
Has anybody seen my love
Has anybody seen my love
I don't know
Has anybody seen my love?

You want to talk to me
Go ahead and talk
Whatever you got to say to me
Won't come as any shock
I must be guilty of something
You just whisper it into my ear
Madame Butterfly
She lulled me to sleep
In a town without pity
Where the water runs deep
She said, "Be easy, baby
There ain't nothin' worth stealin' in here"

You're the one I've been looking for
You're the one that's got the key
But I can't figure out whether I'm too good for you
Or you're too good for me

Has anybody seen my love
Has anybody seen my love
Has anybody seen my love
I don't know
Has anybody seen my love?

Well, they're not showing any lights tonight
And there's no moon
There's just a hot-blooded singer
Singing "Memphis in June"
While they're beatin' the devil out of a guy
Who's wearing a powder-blue wig
Later he'll be shot
For resisting arrest
I can still hear his voice crying
In the wilderness
What looks large from a distance
Close up ain't never that big

Never could learn to drink that blood
And call it wine
Never could learn to hold you, love
And call you mine

DARK EYES

Oh, the gentlemen are talking and the midnight moon is on the riverside
They're drinking up and walking and it is time for me to slide
I live in another world where life and death are memorized
Where the earth is strung with lovers' pearls and all I see are dark eyes

A cock is crowing far away and another soldier's deep in prayer
Some mother's child has gone astray, she can't find him anywhere
But I can hear another drum beating for the dead that rise
Whom nature's beast fears as they come and all I see are dark eyes

They tell me to be discreet for all intended purposes
They tell me revenge is sweet and from where they stand, I'm sure it is
But I feel nothing for their game where beauty goes unrecognized
All I feel is heat and flame and all I see are dark eyes

Oh, the French girl, she's in paradise and a drunken man is at the wheel
Hunger pays a heavy price to the falling gods of speed and steel
Oh, time is short and the days are sweet and passion rules the arrow that flies
A million faces at my feet but all I see are dark eyes

BROWNSVILLE GIRL

(with Sam Shepard)

Well, there was this movie I seen one time
About a man riding 'cross the desert and it starred Gregory Peck
He was shot down by a hungry kid trying to make a name for himself
The townspeople wanted to crush that kid down and string him up by the neck

Well, the marshal, now he beat that kid to a bloody pulp
As the dying gunfighter lay in the sun and gasped for his last breath
"Turn him loose, let him go, let him say he outdrew me fair and square
I want him to feel what it's like to every moment face his death"

Well, I keep seeing this stuff and it just comes a-rolling in
And you know it blows right through me like a ball and chain
You know I can't believe we've lived so long and are still so far apart
The memory of you keeps callin' after me like a rollin' train

I can still see the day that you came to me on the painted desert
In your busted down Ford and your platform heels
I could never figure out why you chose that particular place to meet
Ah, but you were right. It was perfect as I got in behind the wheel

Well, we drove that car all night into San Anton'
And we slept near the Alamo, your skin was so tender and soft
Way down in Mexico you went out to find a doctor and you never came back
I would have gone on after you but I didn't feel like letting my head get blown off

Well, we're drivin' this car and the sun is comin' up over the Rockies
Now I know she ain't you but she's here and she's got that dark rhythm in her soul
But I'm too over the edge and I ain't in the mood anymore to remember the times
    when I was your only man
And she don't want to remind me. She knows this car would go out of control

Brownsville girl with your Brownsville curls
Teeth like pearls shining like the moon above
Brownsville girl, show me all around the world
Brownsville girl, you're my honey love

Well, we crossed the panhandle and then we headed towards Amarillo
We pulled up where Henry Porter used to live. He owned a wreckin' lot
    outside of town about a mile
Ruby was in the backyard hanging clothes, she had her red hair tied back.
    She saw us come rolling up in a trail of dust
She said, "Henry ain't here but you can come on in, he'll be back in a little while"

Then she told us how times were tough and about how she was thinkin' of
    bummin' a ride back to from where she started
But ya know, she changed the subject every time money came up
She said, "Welcome to the land of the living dead."
    You could tell she was so broken hearted
She said, "Even the swap meets around here are getting pretty corrupt"

"How far are y'all going?" Ruby asked us with a sigh
"We're going all the way 'til the wheels fall off and burn
'Til the sun peels the paint and the seat covers fade and the water moccasin dies"
Ruby just smiled and said, "Ah, you know some babies never learn"

Something about that movie though, well I just can't get it out of my head
But I can't remember why I was in it or what part I was supposed to play
All I remember about it was Gregory Peck and the way people moved
And a lot of them seemed to be lookin' my way

Brownsville girl with your Brownsville curls
Teeth like pearls shining like the moon above
Brownsville girl, show me all around the world
Brownsville girl, you're my honey love

Well, they were looking for somebody with a pompadour
I was crossin' the street when shots rang out
I didn't know whether to duck or to run, so I ran
"We got him cornered in the churchyard," I heard somebody shout

Well, you saw my picture in the *Corpus Christi Tribune*. Underneath it,
    it said, "A man with no alibi"
You went out on a limb to testify for me, you said I was with you
Then when I saw you break down in front of the judge and cry real tears
It was the best acting I saw anybody do

Now I've always been the kind of person that doesn't like to trespass
    but sometimes you just find yourself over the line
Oh if there's an original thought out there, I could use it right now
You know, I feel pretty good, but that ain't sayin' much. I could feel a whole lot better
If you were just here by my side to show me how

Well, I'm standin' in line in the rain to see a movie starring Gregory Peck
Yeah, but you know it's not the one that I had in mind
He's got a new one out now, I don't even know what it's about
But I'll see him in anything so I'll stand in line

Brownsville girl with your Brownsville curls
Teeth like pearls shining like the moon above
Brownsville girl, show me all around the world
Brownsville girl, you're my honey love

You know, it's funny how things never turn out the way you had 'em planned
The only thing we knew for sure about Henry Porter is that his name wasn't Henry Porter
And you know there was somethin' about you baby that I liked
    that was always too good for this world
Just like you always said there was somethin' about me you liked
    that I left behind in the French Quarter

Strange how people who suffer together have stronger connections
    than people who are most content
I don't have any regrets, they can talk about me plenty when I'm gone
You always said people don't do what they believe in,
    they just do what's most convenient, then they repent
And I always said, "Hang on to me, baby, and let's hope that the roof stays on"

There was a movie I seen one time, I think I sat through it twice
I don't remember who I was or where I was bound
All I remember about it was it starred Gregory Peck, he wore a gun
    and he was shot in the back
Seems like a long time ago, long before the stars were torn down

Brownsville girl with your Brownsville curls
Teeth like pearls shining like the moon above
Brownsville girl, show me all around the world
Brownsville girl, you're my honey love

EVERYTHING IS BROKEN

Broken lines, broken strings
Broken threads, broken springs
Broken idols, broken heads
People sleeping in broken beds
Ain't no use jiving, ain't no use joking
Everything is broken

Broken bottles, broken plates
Broken switches, broken gates
Broken dishes, broken parts
Streets are filled with broken hearts
Broken words never meant to be spoken
Everything is broken

Seem like every time you stop and turn around
Something else just hit the ground

Broken cutters, broken saws
Broken buckles, broken laws
Broken bodies, broken bones
Broken voices on broken phones
Take a deep breath, feel like you're chokin'
Everything is broken

Every time you leave and go off someplace
Things fall to pieces in my face

Broken hands on broken ploughs
Broken treaties, broken vows
Broken pipes, broken tools
People bending broken rules
Hound dog howling, bullfrog croaking
Everything is broken

RING THEM BELLS

Ring them bells, ye heathen
From the city that dreams
Ring them bells from the sanctuaries
'Cross the valleys and streams
For they're deep and they're wide
And the world's on its side
And time is running backwards
And so is the bride

Ring them bells St. Peter
Where the four winds blow
Ring them bells with an iron hand
So the people will know
Oh it's rush hour now
On the wheel and the plow
And the sun is going down
Upon the sacred cow

Ring them bells Sweet Martha
For the poor man's son
Ring them bells so the world will know
That God is one
Oh the shepherd is asleep
Where the willows weep
And the mountains are filled
With lost sheep

Ring them bells for the blind and the deaf
Ring them bells for all of us who are left
Ring them bells for the chosen few
Who will judge the many when the game is through
Ring them bells, for the time that flies
For the child that cries
When innocence dies

Ring them bells St. Catherine
From the top of the room
Ring them from the fortress
For the lilies that bloom
Oh the lines are long
And the fighting is strong
And they're breaking down the distance
Between right and wrong

SHOOTING STAR

Seen a shooting star tonight
And I thought of you
You were trying to break into another world
A world I never knew
I always kind of wondered
If you ever made it through
Seen a shooting star tonight
And I thought of you

Seen a shooting star tonight
And I thought of me
If I was still the same
If I ever became what you wanted me to be
Did I miss the mark or overstep the line
That only you could see?
Seen a shooting star tonight
And I thought of me

Listen to the engine, listen to the bell
As the last fire truck from hell
Goes rolling by
All good people are praying
It's the last temptation, the last account
The last time you might hear the sermon on the mount
The last radio is playing

Seen a shooting star tonight
Slip away
Tomorrow will be
Another day
Guess it's too late to say the things to you
That you needed to hear me say
Seen a shooting star tonight
Slip away

DIGNITY

Fat man lookin' in a blade of steel
Thin man lookin' at his last meal
Hollow man lookin' in a cottonfield
For dignity

Wise man lookin' in a blade of grass
Young man lookin' in the shadows that pass
Poor man lookin' through painted glass
For dignity

Somebody got murdered on New Year's Eve
Somebody said dignity was the first to leave
I went into the city, went into the town
Went into the land of the midnight sun

Searchin' high, searchin' low
Searchin' everywhere I know
Askin' the cops wherever I go
Have you seen dignity?

Blind man breakin' out of a trance
Puts both his hands in the pockets of chance
Hopin' to find one circumstance
Of dignity

I went to the wedding of Mary Lou
She said, "I don't want nobody see me talkin' to you"
Said she could get killed if she told me what she knew
About dignity

I went down where the vultures feed
I would've gone deeper, but there wasn't any need
Heard the tongues of angels and the tongues of men
Wasn't any difference to me

Chilly wind sharp as a razor blade
House on fire, debts unpaid
Gonna stand at the window, gonna ask the maid
Have you seen dignity?

Drinkin' man listens to the voice he hears
In a crowded room full of covered-up mirrors
Lookin' into the lost forgotten years
For dignity

Met Prince Phillip at the home of the blues
Said he'd give me information if his name wasn't used
He wanted money up front, said he was abused
By dignity

Footprints runnin' 'cross the silver sand
Steps goin' down into tattoo land
I met the sons of darkness and the sons of light
In the bordertowns of despair

Got no place to fade, got no coat
I'm on the rollin' river in a jerkin' boat
Tryin' to read a note somebody wrote
About dignity

Sick man lookin' for the doctor's cure
Lookin' at his hands for the lines that were
And into every masterpiece of literature
For dignity

Englishman stranded in the blackheart wind
Combin' his hair back, his future looks thin
Bites the bullet and he looks within
For dignity

Someone showed me a picture and I just laughed
Dignity never been photographed
I went into the red, went into the black
Into the valley of dry bone dreams

So many roads, so much at stake
So many dead ends, I'm at the edge of the lake
Sometimes I wonder what it's gonna take
To find dignity

SERIES OF DREAMS

I was thinking of a series of dreams
Where nothing comes up to the top
Everything stays down where it's wounded
And comes to a permanent stop
Wasn't thinking of anything specific
Like in a dream, when someone wakes up and screams
Nothing too very scientific
Just thinking of a series of dreams

Thinking of a series of dreams
Where the time and the tempo fly
And there's no exit in any direction
'Cept the one that you can't see with your eyes
Wasn't making any great connection
Wasn't falling for any intricate scheme
Nothing that would pass inspection
Just thinking of a series of dreams

Dreams where the umbrella is folded
Into the path you are hurled
And the cards are no good that you're holding
Unless they're from another world

In one, numbers were burning
In another, I witnessed a crime
In one, I was running, and in another
All I seemed to be doing was climb
Wasn't looking for any special assistance
Not going to any great extremes
I'd already gone the distance
Just thinking of a series of dreams

BORN IN TIME

In the lonely night
In the blinking stardust of a pale blue light
You're comin' thru to me in black and white
When we were made of dreams

You're blowing down the shaky street
You're hearing my heart beat
In the record-breaking heat
Where we were born in time

Not one more night, not one more kiss
Not this time baby, no more of this
Takes too much skill, takes too much will
It's revealing
You came, you saw, just like the law
You married young, just like your ma
You tried and tried, you made me slide
You left me reelin' with this feelin'

On the rising curve
Where the ways of nature will test every nerve
You won't get anything you don't deserve
Where we were born in time

You pressed me once, you pressed me twice
You hang the flame, you'll pay the price
Oh babe, that fire
Is still smokin'
You were snow, you were rain
You were striped, you were plain
Oh babe, truer words
Have not been spoken or broken

In the hills of mystery
In the foggy web of destiny
You can have what's left of me
Where we were born in time

STANDING IN THE DOORWAY

I'm walking through the summer nights
Jukebox playing low
Yesterday everything was going too fast
Today, it's moving too slow
I got no place left to turn
I got nothing left to burn
Don't know if I saw you, if I would kiss you or kill you
It probably wouldn't matter to you anyhow
You left me standing in the doorway crying
I got nothing to go back to now

The light in this place is so bad
Making me sick in the head
All the laughter is just making me sad
The stars have turned cherry red
I'm strumming on my gay guitar
Smoking a cheap cigar
The ghost of our old love has not gone away
Don't look like it will anytime soon
You left me standing in the doorway crying
Under the midnight moon

Maybe they'll get me and maybe they won't
But not tonight and it won't be here
There are things I could say but I don't
I know the mercy of God must be near
I've been riding the midnight train
Got ice water in my veins
I would be crazy if I took you back
It would go up against every rule
You left me standing in the doorway crying
Suffering like a fool

When the last rays of daylight go down
Buddy, you'll roll no more
I can hear the church bells ringing in the yard
I wonder who they're ringing for
I know I can't win
But my heart just won't give in
Last night I danced with a stranger
But she just reminded me you were the one
You left me standing in the doorway crying
In the dark land of the sun

I'll eat when I'm hungry, drink when I'm dry
And live my life on the square
And even if the flesh falls off of my face
I know someone will be there to care
It always means so much
Even the softest touch
I see nothing to be gained by any explanation
There are no words that need to be said
You left me standing in the doorway crying
Blues wrapped around my head

TRYIN' TO GET TO HEAVEN

The air is getting hotter
There's a rumbling in the skies
I've been wading through the high muddy water
With the heat rising in my eyes
Every day your memory grows dimmer
It doesn't haunt me like it did before
I've been walking through the middle of nowhere
Trying to get to heaven before they close the door

When I was in Missouri
They would not let me be
I had to leave there in a hurry
I only saw what they let me see
You broke a heart that loved you
Now you can seal up the book and not write anymore
I've been walking that lonesome valley
Trying to get to heaven before they close the door

People on the platforms
Waiting for the trains
I can hear their hearts a-beatin'
Like pendulums swinging on chains
I tried to give you everything
That your heart was longing for
I'm just going down the road feeling bad
Trying to get to heaven before they close the door

I'm going down the river
Down to New Orleans
They tell me everything is gonna be all right
But I don't know what "all right" even means
I was riding in a buggy with Miss Mary-Jane
Miss Mary-Jane got a house in Baltimore
I been all around the world, boys
Now I'm trying to get to heaven before they close the door

Gonna sleep down in the parlor
And relive my dreams
I'll close my eyes and I wonder
If everything is as hollow as it seems
When you think that you've lost everything
You find out you can always lose a little more
I been to Sugar Town, I shook the sugar down
Now I'm trying to get to heaven before they close the door

MAKE YOU FEEL MY LOVE

When the rain is blowing in your face
And the whole world is on your case
I could offer you a warm embrace
To make you feel my love

When the evening shadows and the stars appear
And there is no one there to dry your tears
I could hold you for a million years
To make you feel my love

I know you haven't made your mind up yet
But I would never do you wrong
I've known it from the moment that we met
No doubt in my mind where you belong

I'd go hungry, I'd go black and blue
I'd go crawling down the avenue
There's nothing that I wouldn't do
To make you feel my love

The storms are raging on the rollin' sea
And on the highway of regret
Put your hand in mine and come with me
I'll see that you don't get wet

I could make you happy, make your dreams come true
Nothing that I wouldn't do
Go to the ends of the earth for you
To make you feel my love

HIGHLANDS

Well my heart's in the Highlands, gentle and fair
Honeysuckle blooming in the wildwood air
Bluebells blazing where the Aberdeen waters flow
Well my heart's in the Highlands
I'm gonna go there when I feel good enough to go

Windows were shakin' all night in my dreams
Everything was exactly the way that it seems
Woke up this morning and I looked at the same old page
Same ol' rat race
Life in the same ol' cage

I don't want nothing from anyone, ain't that much to take
Wouldn't know the difference between a real blonde and a fake
Feel like a prisoner in a world of mystery
I wish someone would come
And push back the clock for me

Well my heart's in the Highlands wherever I roam
That's where I'll be when I get called home
The wind, it whispers to the buck-eyed trees in rhyme
Well my heart's in the Highlands
I can only get there one step at a time

I'm listening to Neil Young, I gotta turn up the sound
Someone's always yelling turn it down
Feel like I'm drifting
Drifting from scene to scene
I'm wondering what in the devil could it all possibly mean?

Insanity is smashing up against my soul
You can say I was on anything but a roll
If I had a conscience, well, I just might blow my top
What would I do with it anyway
Maybe take it to the pawn shop

My heart's in the Highlands at the break of dawn
By the beautiful lake of the Black Swan
Big white clouds like chariots that swing down low
Well my heart's in the Highlands
Only place left to go

I'm in Boston town, in some restaurant
I got no idea what I want
Well, maybe I do but I'm just really not sure
Waitress comes over
Nobody in the place but me and her

It must be a holiday, there's nobody around
She studies me closely as I sit down
She got a pretty face and long white shiny legs
She says, "What'll it be?"
I say, "I don't know, you got any soft boiled eggs?"

She looks at me, says, "I'd bring you some
But we're out of 'm, you picked the wrong time to come"
Then she says, "I know you're an artist, draw a picture of me!"
I say, "I would if I could, but
I don't do sketches from memory"

"Well," she says, "I'm right here in front of you, or haven't you looked?"
I say, "All right, I know, but I don't have my drawing book!"
She gives me a napkin, she says, "You can do it on that"
I say, "Yes I could, but
I don't know where my pencil is at!"

She pulls one out from behind her ear
She says, "All right now, go ahead, draw me, I'm standing right here"
I make a few lines and I show it for her to see
Well she takes the napkin and throws it back
And says, "That don't look a thing like me!"

I said, "Oh, kind Miss, it most certainly does".
She says, "You must be jokin'." I say, "I wish I was!"
Then she says, "You don't read women authors, do you?"
Least that's what I think I hear her say
"Well," I say, "how would you know and what would it matter anyway?"

"Well," she says, "you just don't seem like you do!"
I said, "You're way wrong"
She says, "Which ones have you read then?" I say, "I read Erica Jong!"
She goes away for a minute
And I slide up out of my chair
I step outside back to the busy street but nobody's going anywhere

Well my heart's in the Highlands with the horses and hounds
Way up in the border country, far from the towns
With the twang of the arrow and a snap of the bow
My heart's in the Highlands
Can't see any other way to go

Every day is the same thing out the door
Feel further away than ever before
Some things in life, it gets too late to learn
Well, I'm lost somewhere
I must have made a few bad turns

I see people in the park forgetting their troubles and woes
They're drinking and dancing, wearing bright-colored clothes
All the young men with their young women looking so good
Well, I'd trade places with any of them
In a minute, if I could

I'm crossing the street to get away from a mangy dog
Talking to myself in a monologue
I think what I need might be a full-length leather coat
Somebody just asked me
If I registered to vote

The sun is beginning to shine on me
But it's not like the sun that used to be
The party's over and there's less and less to say
I got new eyes
Everything looks far away

Well, my heart's in the Highlands at the break of day
Over the hills and far away
There's a way to get there and I'll figure it out somehow
But I'm already there in my mind
And that's good enough for now

THINGS HAVE CHANGED

A worried man with a worried mind
No one in front of me and nothing behind
There's a woman on my lap and she's drinking champagne
Got white skin, blood in my eyes
I'm looking up into the sapphire-tinted skies
I'm well dressed, waiting on the last train

Standing on the gallows with my head in a noose
Any minute now I'm expecting all hell to break loose

People are crazy and times are strange
I'm locked in tight, I'm out of range
I used to care, but things have changed

This place ain't doing me any good
I'm in the wrong town, I should be in Hollywood
Just for a second there I thought I saw something move
Gonna take dancing lessons, do the jitterbug rag
Ain't no shortcuts, gonna dress in drag
Only a fool in here would think he's got anything to prove

Lot of water under the bridge, lot of other stuff too
Don't get up gentlemen, I'm only passing through

People are crazy and times are strange
I'm locked in tight, I'm out of range
I used to care, but things have changed

I've been walking forty miles of bad road
If the Bible is right, the world will explode
I've been trying to get as far away from myself as I can
Some things are too hot to touch
The human mind can only stand so much
You can't win with a losing hand

Feel like falling in love with the first woman I meet
Putting her in a wheelbarrow and wheeling her down the street

People are crazy and times are strange
I'm locked in tight, I'm out of range
I used to care, but things have changed

I hurt easy, I just don't show it
You can hurt someone and not even know it
The next sixty seconds could be like an eternity
Gonna get low down, gonna fly high
All the truth in the world adds up to one big lie
I'm in love with a woman who don't even appeal to me

Mr. Jinx and Miss Lucy, they jumped in the lake
I'm not that eager to make a mistake

People are crazy and times are strange
I'm locked in tight, I'm out of range
I used to care, but things have changed

MISSISSIPPI

Every step of the way we walk the line
Your days are numbered, so are mine
Time is pilin' up, we struggle and we scrape
We're all boxed in, nowhere to escape
City's just a jungle, more games to play
Trapped in the heart of it, trying to get away
I was raised in the country, I been workin' in the town
I been in trouble ever since I set my suitcase down
Got nothing for you, I had nothing before
Don't even have anything for myself anymore
Sky full of fire, pain pourin' down
Nothing you can sell me, I'll see you around
All my powers of expression and thoughts so sublime
Could never do you justice in reason or rhyme
Only one thing I did wrong
Stayed in Mississippi a day too long

Well, the devil's in the alley, mule's in the stall
Say anything you wanna, I have heard it all
I was thinkin' about the things that Rosie said
I was dreaming I was sleeping in Rosie's bed
Walking through the leaves, falling from the trees
Feeling like a stranger nobody sees
So many things that we never will undo
I know you're sorry, I'm sorry too
Some people will offer you their hand and some won't
Last night I knew you, tonight I don't
I need somethin' strong to distract my mind
I'm gonna look at you 'til my eyes go blind
Well I got here following the southern star
I crossed that river just to be where you are
Only one thing I did wrong
Stayed in Mississippi a day too long

Well my ship's been split to splinters and it's sinking fast
I'm drownin' in the poison, got no future, got no past
But my heart is not weary, it's light and it's free
I've got nothin' but affection for all those who've sailed with me
Everybody movin' if they ain't already there
Everybody got to move somewhere
Stick with me baby, stick with me anyhow
Things should start to get interesting right about now
My clothes are wet, tight on my skin
Not as tight as the corner that I painted myself in
I know that fortune is waitin' to be kind
So give me your hand and say you'll be mine
Well, the emptiness is endless, cold as the clay
You can always come back, but you can't come back all the way
Only one thing I did wrong
Stayed in Mississippi a day too long

FLOATER (TOO MUCH TO ASK)

Down over the window
Comes the dazzling sunlit rays
Through the back alleys—through the blinds
Another one of them endless days
Honey bees are buzzin'
Leaves begin to stir
I'm in love with my second cousin
I tell myself I could be happy forever with her
I keep listenin' for footsteps
But I ain't hearing any
From the boat I fish for bullheads
I catch a lot, sometimes too many
A summer breeze is blowing
A squall is settin' in
Sometimes it's just plain stupid
To get into any kind of wind

The old men 'round here, sometimes they get
On bad terms with the younger men
But old, young, age don't carry weight
It doesn't matter in the end
One of the boss' hangers-on
Comes to call at times you least expect
Try to bully ya—strong arm you—inspire you with fear
It has the opposite effect
There's a new grove of trees on the outskirts of town
The old one is long gone
Timber two-foot six across
Burns with the bark still on
They say times are hard, if you don't believe it
You can just follow your nose
It don't bother me—times are hard everywhere
We'll just have to see how it goes

My old man, he's like some feudal lord
Got more lives than a cat
Never seen him quarrel with my mother even once
Things come alive or they fall flat
You can smell the pinewood burnin'
You can hear the school bell ring
Gotta get up near the teacher if you can
If you wanna learn anything
Romeo, he said to Juliet, "You got a poor complexion.
It doesn't give your appearance a very youthful touch!"
Juliet said back to Romeo, "Why don't you just shove off
If it bothers you so much."
They all got out of here any way they could
The cold rain can give you the shivers
They went down the Ohio, the Cumberland, the Tennessee
All the rest of them rebel rivers

If you ever try to interfere with me or cross my path again
You do so at the peril of your own life
I'm not quite as cool or forgiving as I sound
I've seen enough heartaches and strife
My grandfather was a duck trapper
He could do it with just dragnets and ropes
My grandmother could sew new dresses out of old cloth
I don't know if they had any dreams or hopes
I had 'em once though, I suppose, to go along
With all the ring dancin' Christmas carols on all of the Christmas Eves
I left all my dreams and hopes
Buried under tobacco leaves
It's not always easy kicking someone out
Gotta wait a while—it can be an unpleasant task
Sometimes somebody wants you to give something up
And tears or not, it's too much to ask

HIGH WATER
(FOR CHARLEY PATTON)

High water risin'—risin' night and day
All the gold and silver are being stolen away
Big Joe Turner lookin' east and west
From the dark room of his mind
He made it to Kansas City
Twelfth Street and Vine
Nothing standing there
High water everywhere

High water risin', the shacks are slidin' down
Folks lose their possessions—folks are leaving town
Bertha Mason shook it—broke it
Then she hung it on a wall
Says, "You're dancin' with whom they tell you to
Or you don't dance at all."
It's tough out there
High water everywhere

I got a cravin' love for blazing speed
Got a hopped up Mustang Ford
Jump into the wagon, love, throw your panties overboard
I can write you poems, make a strong man lose his mind
I'm no pig without a wig
I hope you treat me kind
Things are breakin' up out there
High water everywhere

High water risin', six inches 'bove my head
Coffins droppin' in the street
Like balloons made out of lead
Water pourin' into Vicksburg, don't know what I'm going to do
"Don't reach out for me," she said
"Can't you see I'm drownin' too?"
It's rough out there
High water everywhere

Well, George Lewis told the Englishman, the Italian and the Jew
"Don't open up your mind, boys,
To every conceivable point of view."
They got Charles Darwin trapped out there on Highway Five
Judge says to the High Sheriff
"I want him dead or alive
Either one, I don't care."
High water everywhere

The Cuckoo is a pretty bird, she warbles as she flies
I'm preachin' the word of God
I'm puttin' out your eyes
I asked Fat Nancy for something to eat, she said, "Take it off the shelf—
As great as you are, man,
You'll never be greater than yourself."
I told her I didn't really care
High water everywhere

I'm gettin' up in the morning—I believe I'll dust my broom
Keeping away from the women
I'm givin' 'em lots of room
Thunder rolling over Clarksdale, everything is looking blue
I just can't be happy, love
Unless you're happy too
It's bad out there
High water everywhere

'CROSS THE GREEN MOUNTAIN

(from the film *Gods and Generals*)

I crossed the green mountain, I slept by the stream
Heaven blazin' in my head, I dreamt a monstrous dream
Something came up out of the sea
Swept through the land of the rich and the free

I look into the eyes of my merciful friend
And then I ask myself, is this the end?
Memories linger, sad yet sweet
And I think of the souls in heaven who will meet

Altars are burning with flames falling wide
The foe has crossed over from the other side
They tip their caps from the top of the hill
You can feel them come, more brave blood to spill

Along the dim Atlantic line
The ravaged land lies for miles behind
The light's comin' forward and the streets are broad
All must yield to the avenging God

The world is old, the world is gray
Lessons of life can't be learned in a day
I watch and I wait and I listen while I stand
To the music that comes from a far better land

Close the eyes of our Captain, peace may he know
His long night is done, the great leader is laid low
He was ready to fall, he was quick to defend
Killed outright he was by his own men

It's the last day's last hour of the last happy year
I feel that the unknown world is so near
Pride will vanish and glory will rot
But virtue lives and cannot be forgot

The bells of evening have rung
There's blasphemy on every tongue
Let them say that I walked in fair nature's light
And that I was loyal to truth and to right

Serve God and be cheerful, look upward beyond
Beyond the darkness that masks the surprises of dawn
In the deep green grasses of the blood stained wood
They never dreamed of surrendering. They fell where they stood

Stars fell over Alabama, I saw each star
You're walkin' in dreams whoever you are
Chilled are the skies, keen is the frost
The ground's froze hard and the morning is lost

A letter to mother came today
Gunshot wound to the breast is what it did say
But he'll be better soon he's in a hospital bed
But he'll never be better, he's already dead

I'm ten miles outside the city and I'm lifted away
In an ancient light that is not of day
They were calm, they were blunt, we knew 'em all too well
We loved each other more than we ever dared to tell

THUNDER ON THE MOUNTAIN

Thunder on the mountain, fires on the moon
There's a ruckus in the alley and the sun will be here soon
Today's the day, gonna grab my trombone and blow
Well, there's hot stuff here and it's everywhere I go
I was thinkin' 'bout Alicia Keys, couldn't keep from crying
When she was born in Hell's Kitchen, I was living down the line
I'm wondering where in the world Alicia Keys could be
I been looking for her even clear through Tennessee
Feel like my soul is beginning to expand
Look into my heart and you will sort of understand
You brought me here, now you're trying to run me away
The writing's on the wall, come read it, come see what it say

Thunder on the mountain, rolling like a drum
Gonna sleep over there, that's where the music coming from
I don't need any guide, I already know the way
Remember this, I'm your servant both night and day
The pistols are poppin' and the power is down
I'd like to try somethin' but I'm so far from town
The sun keeps shinin' and the North Wind keeps picking up speed
Gonna forget about myself for a while, gonna go out and see what others need
I've been sitting down studying the art of love
I think it will fit me like a glove
I want some real good woman to do just what I say
Everybody got to wonder what's the matter with this cruel world today

Thunder on the mountain rolling to the ground
Gonna get up in the morning walk the hard road down
Some sweet day I'll stand beside my king
I wouldn't betray your love or any other thing
Gonna raise me an army, some tough sons of bitches
I'll recruit my army from the orphanages
I been to St. Herman's church and I've said my religious vows
I've sucked the milk out of a thousand cows
I got the porkchops, she got the pie
She ain't no angel and neither am I
Shame on your greed, shame on your wicked schemes
I'll say this, I don't give a damn about your dreams

Thunder on the mountain heavy as can be
Mean old twister bearing down on me
All the ladies of Washington scrambling to get out of town
Looks like something bad gonna happen, better roll your airplane down
Everybody's going and I want to go too
Don't wanna take a chance with somebody new
I did all I could and I did it right there and then
I've already confessed——no need to confess again
Gonna make a lot of money, gonna go up north
I'll plant and I'll harvest what the earth brings forth
The hammer's on the table, the pitchfork's on the shelf
For the love of God, you ought to take pity on yourself

WORKINGMAN'S BLUES #2

There's an evening's haze settling over the town
Starlight by the edge of the creek
The buying power of the proletariat's gone down
Money's getting shallow and weak
The place I love best is a sweet memory
It's a new path that we trod
They say low wages are a reality
If we want to compete abroad

My cruel weapons been laid back on the shelf
Come and sit down on my knee
You are dearer to me than myself
As you yourself can see
I'm listening to the steel rails hum
Got both eyes tight shut
I'm just trying to keep the hunger from
Creepin' its way into my gut

Meet me at the bottom, don't lag behind
Bring me my boots and shoes
You can hang back or fight your best on the front line
Sing a little bit of these workingman's blues

I'm sailing on back getting ready for the long haul
Leaving everything behind
If I stay here I'll lose it all
The bandits will rob me blind
I'm trying to feed my soul with thought
Gonna sleep off the rest of the day
Sometimes nobody wants what you got
Sometimes you can't give it away

I woke up this morning and sprang to my feet
Went into town on a whim
I saw my father there in the street
At least I think it was him
In the dark I hear the night birds call
The hills are rugged and steep
I sleep in the kitchen with my feet in the hall
If I told you my whole story you'd weep

Meet me at the bottom, don't lag behind
Bring me my boots and shoes
You can hang back or fight your best on the front line
Sing a little bit of these workingman's blues

They burned my barn and they stole my horse
I can't save a dime
It's a long way down and I don't want to be forced
Into a life of continual crime
I can see for myself that the sun is sinking
O'er the banks of the deep blue sea
Tell me, am I wrong in thinking
That you have forgotten me

Now they worry and they hurry and they fuss and they fret
They waste your nights and days
Them, I will forget
You, I'll remember always
It's a cold black night and it's midsummer's eve
And the stars are spinning around
I still find it so hard to believe
That someone would kick me when I'm down

Meet me at the bottom, don't lag behind
Bring me my boots and shoes
You can hang back or fight your best on the front line
Sing a little bit of these workingman's blues

I'll be back home in a month or two
When the frost is on the vine
I'll punch my spear right straight through
Half-ways down your spine
I'll lift up my arms to the starry skies
And pray the fugitive's prayer
I'm guessing tomorrow the sun will rise
I hope the final judgment's fair

The battle is over up in the hills
And the mist is closing in
Look at me, with all of my spoils
What did I ever win?
Gotta brand new suit and a brand new wife
I can live on rice and beans
Some people never worked a day in their life
They don't know what work even means

Meet me at the bottom, don't lag behind
Bring me my boots and shoes
You can hang back or fight your best on the front line
Sing a little bit of these workingman's blues

AIN'T TALKIN'

As I walked out tonight in the mystic garden
The wounded flowers were dangling from the vines
I was passing by yon cool and crystal fountain
Someone hit me from behind

Ain't talkin', just walkin'
Through this weary world of woe
Heart burnin', still yearnin'
No one on earth would ever know

They say prayer has the power to help
So pray for me mother
In the human heart an evil spirit can dwell
I'm trying to love my neighbor and do good unto others
But oh, mother, things ain't going well

Ain't talkin', just walkin'
I'll burn that bridge before you can cross
Heart burnin', still yearnin'
They'll be no mercy for you once you've lost

Now I'm all worn down by weepin'
My eyes are filled with tears, my lips are dry
If I catch my opponents ever sleepin'
I'll just slaughter them where they lie

Ain't talkin', just walkin'
Through a world mysterious and vague
Heart burnin', still yearnin'
Walking through the cities of the plague

The whole world is filled with speculation
The whole wide world which people say is round
They will tear your mind away from contemplation
They will jump on your misfortune when you're down

Ain't talkin', just walkin'
Eatin' hog-eyed grease in hog-eyed town
Heart burnin', still yearnin'
Someday you'll be glad to have me around

They will crush you with wealth and power
Every waking moment you could crack
I'll make the most of one last extra hour
I'll avenge my father's death then I'll step back

Ain't talkin', just walkin'
Hand me down my walkin' cane
Heart burnin', still yearnin'
Got to get you out of my miserable brain

It's bright in the heavens and the wheels are flying
Fame and honor never seem to fade
The fire's gone out but the light is never dying
Who says I can't get heavenly aid?

Ain't talkin', just walkin'
Carrying a dead man's shield
Heart burnin', still yearnin'
Walkin' with a toothache in my heel

The suffering is unending
Every nook and cranny has its tears
I'm not playing, I'm not pretending
I'm not nursing any superfluous fears

Ain't talkin', just walkin'
Walkin' ever since the other night
Heart burnin', still yearnin'
Walkin' 'til I'm clean out of sight

As I walked out in the mystic garden
On a hot summer day, hot summer lawn
Excuse me, ma'am, I beg your pardon
There's no one here, the gardener is gone

Ain't talkin', just walkin'
Up the road around the bend
Heart burnin', still yearnin'
In the last outback, at the world's end

BEYOND HERE LIES NOTHIN'

(with Robert Hunter)

I love you pretty baby
You're the only love I've ever known
Just as long as you stay with me
The whole world is my throne
Beyond here lies nothin'
Nothin' we can call our own

I'm movin' after midnight
Down boulevards of broken cars
Don't know what I'd do without it
Without this love that we call ours
Beyond here lies nothin'
Nothin' but the moon and stars

Down every street there's a window
And every window made of glass
We'll keep on lovin' pretty baby
For as long as love will last
Beyond here lies nothin'
But the mountains of the past

My ship is in the harbor
And the sails are spread
Listen to me pretty baby
Lay your hand upon my head
Beyond here lies nothin'
Nothin' done and nothin' said

THIS DREAM OF YOU

How long can I stay in this nowhere café
'Fore night turns into day
I wonder why I'm so frightened of dawn
All I have and all I know
Is this dream of you
Which keeps me living on

There's a moment when all old things
Become new again
But that moment might have been here and gone
All I have and all I know
Is this dream of you
Which keeps me living on

I look away, but I keep seeing it
I don't want to believe, but I keep believing it
Shadows dance upon the wall
Shadows that seem to know it all

Am I too blind to see?
Is my heart playing tricks on me?
Too late to stop now even though all my friends are gone
All I have and all I know
Is this dream of you
Which keeps me living on

Everything I touch seems to disappear
Everywhere I turn you are always here
I'll run this race until my earthly death
I'll defend this place with my dying breath

From a cheerless room in a curtained gloom
I saw a star from heaven fall
I turned and looked again but it was gone
All I have and all I know
Is this dream of you
Which keeps me living on

LONG AND WASTED YEARS

It's been such a long, long time
Since we loved each other and our hearts were true
One time, for one brief day
I was the man for you

Last night I heard you talking in your sleep
Saying things you shouldn't say
Oh, baby
You just might have to go to jail some day

Is there a place we can go?
Is there anybody we can see?
Maybe what's right for you
Isn't really right for me

I ain't seen my family in twenty years
That ain't easy to understand
They may be dead by now
I lost track of them after they lost their land

Shake it up baby, twist and shout
You tell me what it's all about
What you doing out in the sun anyway?
Don't you know the sun can burn your brains right out?

My enemy slammed into the earth
I don't know what he was worth
But he lost it all, everything and more
What a blithering fool he took me for

I wear dark glasses to cover my eyes
There're secrets in them I can't disguise
Come back, baby
If I hurt your feelings, I apologize

Two trains running side by side
Forty miles wide down the Eastern line
You don't have to go, I just came to you
Because you're a friend of mine

I think when my back was turned
The whole world behind me burned
Maybe today, if not today, maybe tomorrow
Maybe there'll be a limit on all my sorrow

We cried on a cold and frosty morn'
We cried because our souls were torn
So much for tears
So much for those long and wasted years

SCARLET TOWN

In Scarlet Town where I was born
There's ivy leaf and silver thorn
The streets have names you can't pronounce
Gold is down to a quarter of an ounce

The music starts and the people sway
Everybody says, are you going my way?
Uncle Tom still working for Uncle Bill
Scarlet Town is under the hill

Scarlet Town in the month of May
Sweet William on his deathbed lay
Mistress Mary by the side of the bed
Kissing his face, heaping prayers on his head

So brave, so true, so gentle is he
I'll weep for him as he'd weep for me
Little Boy Blue come blow your horn
In Scarlet Town where I was born

Scarlet Town in the hot noon hours
There's palm leaf shadows and scattered flowers
Beggars crouching at the gate
Help comes but it comes too late

On marble slabs and in fields of stone
You make your humble wishes known
I touched the garment but the hem was torn
In Scarlet Town where I was born

In Scarlet Town the end is near
The seven wonders of the world are here
The evil and the good living side by side
All human forms seem glorified

Put your heart on a platter and see who'll bite
See who'll hold you and kiss you good night
There's walnut groves and maple wood
In Scarlet Town crying won't do you no good

In Scarlet Town you fight your father's foes
Up on the hill a chilly wind blows
You fight 'em on high and you fight 'em down in
You fight 'em with whisky, morphine and gin

You got legs that can drive men mad
A lot of things we didn't do that I wish we had
In Scarlet Town the sky is clear
You'll wish to God that you stayed right here

Set 'em up Joe, play Walking The Floor
Play it for my flat chested junkie whore
I'm staying up late and I'm making amends
While the smile of heaven descends

If love is a sin then beauty is a crime
All things are beautiful in their time
The black and the white, the yellow and the brown
It's all right there for ya in Scarlet Town

EARLY ROMAN KINGS

All the early Roman Kings in their sharkskin suits
Bowties and buttons, high top boots
Driving the spikes in, blazing the rails
Nailed in their coffins in top hats and tails
Fly away little bird, fly away, flap your wings
Fly by night like the early Roman Kings

All the early Roman Kings in the early, early morn'
Coming down the mountain, distributing the corn
Speeding through the forest, racing down the track
You try to get away, they drag you back
Tomorrow is Friday, we'll see what it brings
Everybody's talking 'bout the early Roman Kings

They're peddlers and they're meddlers, they buy and they sell
They destroyed your city, they'll destroy you as well
They're lecherous and treacherous, hell bent for leather
Each of them bigger than all men put together
Sluggers and muggers wearing fancy gold rings
All the women going crazy for the early Roman Kings

I'll dress up your wounds with a blood clotted rag
I ain't afraid to make love to a bitch or a hag
If you see me coming and you're standing there
Wave your handkerchief in the air
I ain't dead yet, my bell still rings
I keep my fingers crossed like the early Roman Kings

I'll strip you of life, strip you of breath
Ship you down to the house of death
One day you will ask for me
There'll be no one else that you'll want to see
Bring down my fiddle, tune up my strings
Gonna break it wide open like the early Roman Kings

I was up on black mountain the day Detroit fell
They killed them all off and they sent them to hell
Ding Dong Daddy, you're coming up short
Gonna put you on trial in a Sicilian court
I've had my fun, I've had my flings
Gonna shake 'em all down like the early Roman Kings

I CONTAIN MULTITUDES

Today and tomorrow and yesterday too
The flowers are dying like all things do
Follow me close—I'm going to Bally-Na-Lee
I'll lose my mind if you don't come with me
I fuss with my hair and I fight blood feuds . . . I contain multitudes

Gotta tell tale heart like Mr. Poe
Got skeletons in the walls of people you know
I'll drink to the truth of things that we said
I'll drink to the man that shares your bed
I paint landscapes—I paint nudes . . . I contain multitudes

A red Cadillac and a black moustache
Rings on my fingers that sparkle and flash
Tell me what's next—what shall we do
Half my soul baby belongs to you
I rollick and I frolic with all the young dudes . . . I contain multitudes

I'm just like Anne Frank—like Indiana Jones
And them British bad boys the Rolling Stones
I go right to the edge—I go right to the end
I go right where all things lost—are made good again

I sing the songs of experience like William Blake
I have no apologies to make
Everything's flowin' all at the same time
I live on the boulevard of crime
I drive fast cars and I eat fast foods . . . I contain multitudes

Pink pedal pushers and red blue jeans
All the pretty maids and all the old queens
All the old queens from all my past lives
I carry four pistols and two large knives
I'm a man of contradictions and a man of many moods . . . I contain multitudes

Greedy old wolf——I'll show you my heart
But not all of it——only the hateful part
I'll sell you down the river——I'll put a price on your head
What more can I tell ya——I sleep with life and death in the same bed

Get lost Madam——get up off my knee
Keep your mouth away from me
I'll keep the path open——the path in my mind
I'll see to it that there's no love left behind
I play Beethoven sonatas Chopin's preludes . . . I contain multitudes

MURDER MOST FOUL

'Twas a dark day in Dallas—November '63
The day that will live on in infamy
President Kennedy was riding high
A good day to be living and a good day to die
Being led to the slaughter like a sacrificial lamb
Say wait a minute boys, do you know who I am?
Of course we do, we know who you are
Then they blew off his head when he was still in the car
Shot down like a dog in broad daylight
'Twas a matter of timing and the timing was right
You got unpaid debts and we've come to collect
We're gon' kill you with hatred and without any respect
We'll mock you and shock you, we'll grin in your face
We've already got someone here to take your place
The day that they blew out the brains of the king
Thousands were watching, no one saw a thing
It happened so quickly—so quick by surprise
Right there in front of everyone's eyes

Greatest magic trick ever under the sun
Perfectly executed, skillfully done
Wolfman, oh wolfman, oh wolfman, howl
Rub a dub dub—it's murder most foul

Hush lil children, you'll soon understand
The Beatles are coming they're gonna hold your hand
Slide down the banister, go get your coat
Ferry 'cross the Mersey and go for the throat
There's three bums comin' all dressed in rags
Pick up the pieces and lower the flags
I'm going to Woodstock, it's the Aquarian Age
Then I'll go over to Altamont and sit near the stage
Put your head out the window, let the good times roll
There's a party going on behind the grassy knoll
Stack up the bricks and pour the cement

Don't say Dallas don't love you, Mr. President
Put your foot in the tank and step on the gas
Try to make it to the triple underpass
Black face singer—white face clown
Better not show your faces after the sun goes down

I'm in the red-light district like a cop on the beat
Living in a nightmare on Elm Street
When you're down on Deep Ellum put your money in your shoe
Don't ask what your country can do for you
Cash on the barrel head, money to burn
Dealey Plaza, make a left hand turn
Go down to the crossroads, try to flag a ride
That's the place where Faith, Hope and Charity died
Shoot 'em while he runs, boy, shoot 'em while you can
See if you can shoot the Invisible Man
Goodbye, Charlie, goodbye Uncle Sam
Frankly, Miss Scarlet, I don't give a damn
What is the truth and where did it go
Ask Oswald and Ruby—they oughta know
Shut your mouth, says the wise old owl
Business is business and it's murder most foul

Tommy can you hear me, I'm the Acid Queen
I'm ridin' in a long black Lincoln limousine
Ridin' in the back seat, next to my wife
Heading straight on into the afterlife
I'm leaning to the left, got my head in her lap
Oh Lord, I've been led into some kind of a trap
We ask no quarter, no quarter do we give
We're right down the street from the street where you live
They mutilated his body and took out his brain
What more could they do, they piled on the pain
But his soul was not there where it was supposed to be at
For the last fifty years they've been searching for that
Freedom, oh freedom, freedom over me

Hate to tell you, Mister, but only dead men are free
Send me some loving—tell me no lie
Throw the gun in the gutter and walk on by
Wake up, Little Suzie, let's go for a drive
Cross the Trinity River, let's keep hope alive
Turn the radio on, don't touch the dials
Parkland Hospital's only six more miles
You got me dizzy Miss Lizzy, you filled me with lead
That magic bullet of yours has gone to my head
I'm just a patsy like Patsy Cline
I never shot anyone from in front or behind
Got blood in my eyes, got blood in my ear
I'm never gonna make it to the New Frontier

Zapruder's film, I've seen that before
Seen it thirty three times, maybe more
It's vile and deceitful—it's cruel and it's mean
Ugliest thing that you ever have seen
They killed him once, they killed him twice
Killed him like a human sacrifice
The day that they killed him, someone said to me, "Son,
The age of the anti-Christ has just only begun."
Air Force One coming in through the gate
Johnson sworn in at two thirty-eight
Let me know when you decide to throw in the towel
It is what it is and it's murder most foul

What's New Pussycat—wha'd I say
I said the soul of a nation been torn away
It's beginning to go down into a slow decay
And that it's thirty-six hours past judgment day
Wolfman Jack, he's speaking in tongues
He's going on and on at the top of his lungs
Play me a song, Mr. Wolfman Jack
Play it for me in my long Cadillac
Play that Only The Good Die Young

Take me to the place where Tom Dooley was hung
Play St. James Infirmary in the court of King James
If you want to remember, better write down the names
Play Etta James too, play I'd Rather Go Blind
Play it for the man with the telepathic mind
Play John Lee Hooker play Scratch My Back
Play it for that strip club owner named Jack
Guitar Slim—Goin' Down Slow
Play it for me and for Marilyn Monroe
And please, Don't Let Me Be Misunderstood
Play it for the First Lady, she ain't feeling that good
Play Don Henley—play Glenn Frey
Take it to the Limit and let it go by
And play it for Carl Wilson, too
Lookin' far, far away down Gower Avenue
Play Tragedy, play Twilight Time
Take Me Back to Tulsa to the scene of the crime
Play another one and Another One Bites the Dust
Play the Old Rugged Cross and in G-d We Trust
Ride the Pink Horse down that Long, Lonesome Road
Stand there and wait for his head to explode
Play Mystery Train for Mr. Mystery
The man who fell down dead, like a rootless tree
Play it for the Reverend, play it for the Pastor
Play it for the dog that's got no master
Play Oscar Peterson and play Stan Getz
Play Blue Sky, play Dickie Betts
Play Art Pepper, play Thelonious Monk
Charlie Parker and all that junk
All that junk and All That Jazz
Play something for The Birdman of Alcatraz
Play Buster Keaton play Harold Lloyd
Play Bugsy Siegel play Pretty Boy Floyd
Play all the numbers, play all the odds
Play Cry Me A River for the Lord of the Gods
Play number nine, play number six

Play it for Lindsey and Stevie Nicks
Play Nat King Cole, play Nature Boy
Play Down in the Boondocks for Terry Malloy
Play It Happened One Night and One Night of Sin
There's twelve million souls that are listening in
Play the Merchant of Venice, play the merchants of death
Play Stella by Starlight for Lady Macbeth
Don't worry Mr. President, help's on the way
Your brothers are comin', there'll be hell to pay
Brothers? What brothers? What's this about hell?
Tell 'em we're waitin'—keep coming—we'll get 'em as well
Love Field is where his plane touched down
But it never did get back up off of the ground
Was a hard act to follow, second to none
They killed him on the Altar of the Rising Sun
Play Misty for me and that Old Devil Moon
Play Anything Goes and Memphis in June
Play Lonely at the Top and Lonely Are the Brave
Play it for Houdini spinning around in his grave
Play Jelly Roll Morton, play Lucille
Play Deep in a Dream and play Drivin' Wheel
Play Moonlight Sonata in F sharp
And Key to the Highway by the king of the harp
Play Marchin' Through Georgia and Dumbarton's Drums
Play Darkness and death will come when it comes
Play Love Me or Leave Me by the great Bud Powell
Play the Blood Stained Banner—play Murder Most Foul

INDEX OF PUBLISHERS AND COPYRIGHT DATES